MYTHS OF THE WORLD

NORSE GODS AND HEROES

MYTHS OF THE WORLD

NORSE GODS AND HEROES

MORGAN J. ROBERTS

Friedman Group

A FRIEDMAN GROUP BOOK

Library of Congress Cataloging-in-Publication Data

Roberts, Morgan J., 1970–
    Norse gods and heroes / Morgan J. Roberts
        p. cm. — (Myths of the world)
    Includes bibliographical references (p. 110) and index.
    ISBN 1-56799-090-8
    1. Mythology, Norse. I. Title. II. Series.
BL860.R62 1994   94-10323
293'. 13—dc20   CIP

MYTHS OF THE WORLD: NORSE GODS AND HEROES
was prepared and produced by
Michael Friedman Publishing Group, Inc.
15 West 26th Street
New York, New York 10010

Editor: Nathaniel Marunas
Art Director: Jeff Batzli
Designer: Susan E. Livingston
Photography Editor: Susan Mettler

Color separations by Scantrans Pte. Ltd.
Printed and bound in China by Leefung-Asco Printers Ltd.

PHOTOGRAPHY CREDITS

CM Dixon: 73, 76, 95

©Wenzel Fischer/FPG International: 18

FPG International: 109

Giraudon/Art Resource, New York: 14, 27, 33 top, 106

©Susan Grey/FPG International: 98-99

©Keith Gunnar/FPG International: 16

Historical Pictures/Stock Montage, Inc.: 23, 26, 58, 64

©James McLoughlin/FPG International: 11

The National Museum of Denmark: 45

New York Public Library Map Collection: 12-13

North Wind Picture Archives: 8, 28, 30, 32, 33 bottom, 40,
    53, 108

Siena Artworks, ©Michael Friedman Publishing Group: 46, 54,
    56, 57, 88

©Ulf Sjostedt/FPG International: 15, 36 bottom, 90-91

©Kit Weiss/The National Museum of Denmark: 84

Werner Forman Archive/Art Resource, New York: 2, 6, 19, 20,
    21, 22, 24, 25, 37, 41, 42, 44, 49, 50, 51, 62, 63 bottom,
    67 bottom, 72, 75, 82, 85, 86, 92-93, 93 bottom, 94 bottom,
    96, 101, 102, 103, 104 bottom, 105

DEDICATION

For Amy.

CONTENTS

THE INCONSISTENCY OF NORSE MYTHOLOGY

One of the most frustrating aspects of the Norse canon is that so little original material has survived. The majority of our modern-day knowledge comes from a small collection of documents. The earliest known relevant text, Tacitus' *Germania*, dates from the first century A.D. and contains the first documented mention of ancient Germanic theological beliefs. After this comes the *Codex Regius*, which consists of twenty-nine poems written around 1270 by various uncredited authors. Soon after the discovery of the *Codex Regius*

An Icelandic Scald tells his stories to a group of Vikings. The Scalds were not only the storytellers of the ancient Norse world, but the priests as well.

OPPOSITE: Iceland's forbidding landscape contributed to the development of a people who were hardy and courageous—if somewhat reckless.

BELOW: Odin, the king of the Aesir, sits upon Hlidskialf, surveying the nine worlds. Note the ravens Hugin (thought) and Munin (memory) whispering into his ears.

in Iceland in 1643, the *Arnamagnaean Codex* was found, also in Iceland. It contained five poems very similar in nature to those of the *Regius*, but contained one new poem, "Baldrs Draumar," that dealt with the death of Balder, the god of light. Because of the similar natures of these documents, all thirty-four poems were given the collective title of the *Elder Edda* or *Poetic Edda*. Since this work is an amalgamation of many poets, who were likely separated by hundreds of years, many inconsistencies are present in these myths. Even though the poems in the *Elder Edda* were written by people who believed in the gods and heroes they were writing about, characters in

these works who have already died spring up again out of the blue. Events that have taken place in one poem have yet to take place in another. The origins of the gods and their weaponry vary from poem to poem.

Another, more important source is a text by a man named Snorri Sturluson (1179–1241), the *Prose Edda*. By the time Sturluson began writing, Christianity had taken hold in Iceland. The onset of this new religion was causing the poetic forms of the ancient Scalds, the religious bards of Iceland, to disappear.

Along with the Scaldic style, the stories of the ancient gods were also disappearing. Sturluson took it upon himself to commit to paper not only the poetic techniques of the Scalds but a good number of the most famous ancient myths as well. This stylebook became the *Prose Edda*. (Confusingly, the *Elder Edda* is the more recent work.)

Although Sturluson's work documents a number of myths not told in the *Elder Edda*, it must be kept in mind that he was writing down the myths many centuries after those who originally circulated them had died. Through the course of time many of the myths as they reached Sturluson's ears had undergone structural and narrative changes. Thus, when both the *Elder Edda* and the *Prose Edda* are combined, we are presented with a canon of myths that is rife with inconsistencies and incongruities.

THE FATALISM OF NORSE MYTHOLOGY

Another characteristic of the Norse canon that differentiates it from practically any other ancient canon is its inherent bleakness. The harshness of the barren Icelandic landscape is reflected in the stories and myths of its ancient people.

The Norse gods were a race of half-giant, half-god deities who were not immortal. These deities understood that a time would come when they would meet their own deaths. The mortal nature of these gods reflected the fatalistic mindset in the northern races. If the lives of the ancient Norse seemed surpassingly transient, it makes sense that their pantheon reflected a certain "mortality." The most a Norseman could aspire to was to

This map of Iceland is from a seventeenth-century atlas made by the famous Dutch cartographer and publisher Willem Janszoon Blaeu, who is credited with the invention of a printing press that was the first to feature significant improvements since Gutenberg built the first press in the fifteenth century. With its many fjords, Iceland has always been appealing to map makers.

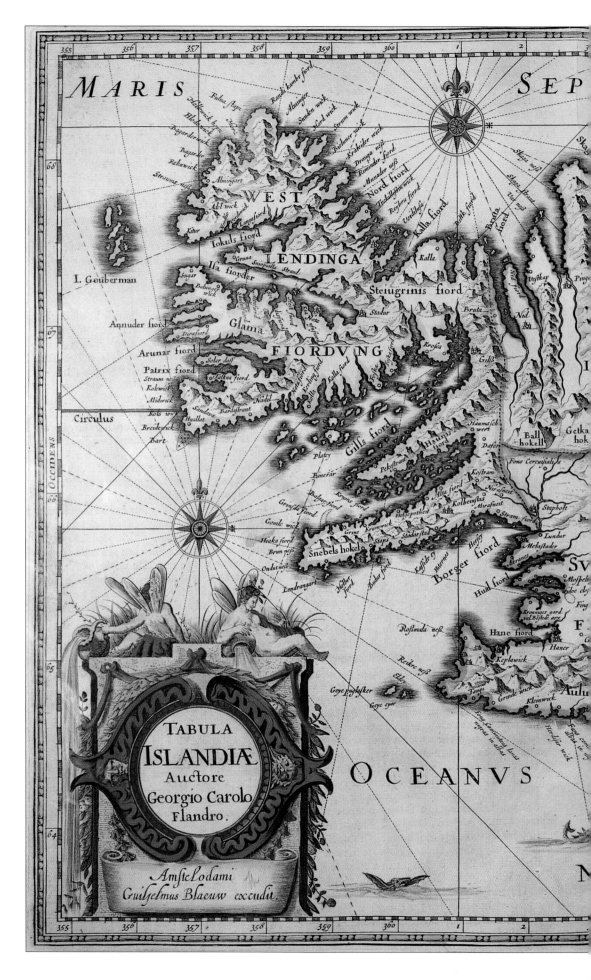

THE INCONSISTENCY OF NORSE MYTHOLOGY

RIGHT: This ninth-century Icelandic artwork depicts the funeral ship of a dead Norse warrior; his comrades are manning the sails.

OPPOSITE: The summers are brief in Iceland, and are therefore most welcome. Not surprisingly, the most benevolent gods in the Norse pantheon were associated with the season or with the sun itself.

die fighting against the world's evils, be those evils in the form of a rival clan, inclement weather, or a pack of wolves.

For the ancient Norsemen, the noblest way to die was in battle, at an early age. By doing this they would be granted a seat in Valhala, the hall of the chosen slain, where they would fight and feast continually until the time of Ragnarok, the apocalypse, when everything in the universe would be destroyed, including the gods themselves. To die of old age or illness was considered cowardly. Since their religion told them nothing was permanent, not even the gods, the ancient Norse thought it only right to fight, violently and until the death, against the evils of the world. And the world of the ancient Norse must have seemed full of evil, where almost everything was against man. The Icelandic landscape was cold and inhospitable, the long months of winter broken by the warming rays of the sun for only a short time every year.

Iceland is situated in such a northerly position that the seasons of winter and summer are delineated by the amount of ambient light in the sky. During the summer the sun never fully sets, making nighttime a perpetual dusk. But during the long winter the darkness is nearly complete. This unrelenting darkness adds to the already harsh wintry climate, making the northern winters times of great hardship. (It is hardly surprising that the malignant characters in the Norse canon were associated with the extreme cold.)

For the ancient Norse the world was characterized by clear delineations of good and evil, light and dark. These delineations made for a mythological canon that represented good and evil as equally balanced forces that were constantly at odds, always trying to tip the scales. It was all an ancient Norseman could do to keep the balance equal by standing firm against the forces of evil, as his gods did, whenever evil arose.

IN
THE BEGINNING

CREATION OF THE GODS, GIANTS,
AND THE UNIVERSE

When the universe was nothing but chaos, darkness, and confusion, there was a gigantic cleft, an abyss, in the center of everything. It was so deep that its bottom was inconceivable. Inside its cragged walls the temperature was so low that it would have instantly frozen a man solid. This abyss was called Ginnungagap.

This icy crevasse in Iceland would be a good model for the frozen splendor of the primordial abyss known as Ginnungagap.

The glacial rivers of Iceland no doubt inspired tales of the Elivagar.

Directly to the north of Ginnungagap was the realm of Niflheim, a dark world shrouded in continual mist. The spring Hvergelmir was in this twilight place, and from it flowed the eleven rivers of Niflheim, known collectively as the Elivagar. Individually, the Elivagar were named Fimbulthul, Fjorm, Gjoll, Gunnthra, Hrid, Leipt, Slid, Svol, Sylg, Vid, and Ylg. These rivers, having nowhere else to go, all eventually flowed into Ginnungagap. As soon as their waters hit the icy air, they froze into gigantic blocks of ice that slowly filled the massive chasm.

To the south of Ginnungagap was Muspellsheim, the world of fire and perpetual light—the opposite of Niflheim in every respect. Here lived Surtr the flame giant, the first living entity, who played a large role not only in the creation of the universe but also in its eventual destruction. It was Surtr's job to protect Muspellsheim from trespassers. But since he was the only living being, he found himself bored most of the time. In his boredom he practiced with his flaming sword, honing his skills, sending great waves of sparks and flame out into the chasm of Ginnungagap. There the fire met the blocks of ice on the abyss floor, sending great torrents of steam upward into the frigid air, where the moisture was frozen again, returning to the chasm floor as frost. From this frost were formed two creatures: Ymir, the primogenitor of the giants, and Audhumbla, an enormous cow.

Naturally, after a while both of these new beings became ravenously hungry. And while Ymir kneaded Audhumbla's udders, supplying himself with rivers of milk, Audhumbla herself had nothing to eat but the frost from the ice. She licked the ice blocks until she uncovered the god Buri, whose name means "producer." This was an apt moniker for the being who would become the grandfather of the Aesir, the ruling gods of Norse mythology.

After gorging himself on Audhumbla's rich milk, Ymir lay down on the chasm's floor to sleep off the slothfulness brought on by overeating. As he dozed unaware of the goings-on around him a sheet of fire from Surtr's sword fell very close to his sleeping body. The warmth both deepened his sleep and made him perspire. From this perspiration was born Thrudgelmir, an ugly six-headed giant who was the grandfather of the frost giants, the sworn enemies of the Aesir. From the sweat of Ymir's armpits came two other children, also giants, though not as malformed as Thrudgelmir. This brother and sister had only one head each, but they were still hideously ugly. Their names were never recorded.

Soon after his birth, Buri produced a son, the god Bor. Bor soon married the giantess Bestla, and with her produced three sons. The first was named Odin, the second Vili, and the third Ve. These children were the first of the race of Aesir, destined to become the ruling forces of good in the Norse universe.

When Thrudgelmir and his young son Bergelmir (who had sprung from his father much in the same way Bor had sprung from Buri) discovered the existence of Bor's children, they quickly enlisted the aid of their brother and sister giants to help them destroy these forces of good.

The war between the children of Thrudgelmir and the children of Bor raged for countless ages in the depths of Ginnungagap with no advantage ever going to either side. The children of Bor, though few in number, were incredibly strong. The wounds they sustained quickly healed; it was impossible to kill them. The giants, while more vulnerable than the children of Bor, kept producing new children to replenish their ranks. For thousands of years the battle between good and evil continued with neither side showing any sign of weakening or losing ground.

Eventually Odin, Vili, and Ve ambushed and defeated their most hated enemy, the original frost giant Ymir himself, who collapsed to the floor of Ginnungagap, blood flowing furiously from his wounds. It was this flood of Ymir's blood that killed the rest of the giant army, all of whom, save for two, drowned in the blood of their original father.

The giants who survived the flood were Bergelmir and his wife, whose name is unknown. They escaped the flood by piloting a

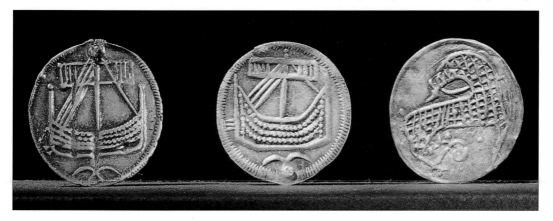

These three Viking coins, which have images of sailing vessels embossed on their surfaces, were found at an ancient Viking marketplace at Birka, located in Sweden.

ship on the ocean of blood, finally settling in a land far to the south, thereafter dubbed Jotunheim, the land of the giants. Here the two created a new race of frost giants, all of whom were taught to hate their vanquishers, the Aesir.

CREATION OF THE WORLD

Now that the war was over, Odin, Vili, and Ve decided it was time to make the universe a more pleasant place. They decided to create a world out of Ymir's corpse (it was all they had from which to fashion a world). Ymir's blood had already formed the oceans. From the corpse's flesh they created Midgard, the earth, which would soon become the home of mankind. This they positioned between themselves and Jotunheim, wanting to put as much distance as possible between themselves and the giants. They used Ymir's bones to prop up loose pockets of flesh, creating hills and valleys. His teeth, jagged and broken, became the world's many cliffs. His hair became the earth's vegetation. His skull became the heavens above. And whatever brains were left in his skull after the massacre became the billowing, primordial clouds.

With the earth and sky now in place the gods decided that a light was needed. They traveled to Muspellsheim to collect some of the sparks that flew from Surtr's blade. They threw these pieces of undying fire into the sky, where they became the stars. Out of all the sparks there were two that outshone the rest; these became the sun and moon.

The gods fashioned two chariots, built specifically for hauling these two magnificent orbs across the sky. The sun chariot was equipped with the safety and comfort of both the steeds and driver in mind. Pouches of ice

were secured behind the horses, protecting their hindquarters from the awesome heat of the sun. They also created the shield Svalin to protect both driver and steeds from the undying rays. The moon chariot did not have to be outfitted with the same safety precautions since the moon's rays were not as fierce as the sun's. The horses Arvakr, "the early riser," and Alsvin, "the quick-footed," were chosen to pull the sun chariot across the sky. Arvakr ensured that the sun rose early in the day and Alsvin made certain it wouldn't linger too long over Midgard and scorch it. The moon chariot's steed was named Alsvider, which means "always quick."

During the great war between the giants and the Aesir, numerous relationships between the two races had developed, despite their ongoing feud. Aesir became intimate with giants and giants became intimate with Aesir. Numerous children were conceived, many of whom would later become important characters in the canon. Two such children were Mani and Sol, whose names mean, respectively, "moon" and "sun." They had been so named because their father thought they were as beautiful as the orbs fetched from Muspellsheim. When searching for drivers for the chariots, Odin took notice of the pair and knew he had found the appropriate charioteers. Every day Mani and Sol drove the moon and sun across the sky, creating not only day and night, but time as well. As with everything in the Norse canon, however, such beneficence could not go unchallenged.

Quick on the heels of both Mani and Sol during their daily rides across the sky were the wolves Skoll and Hati. These ravenous beasts were possessed by a singular desire: to overtake and swallow the magnificent glowing orbs in the sky. Only at the time of Ragnarok, when all would be destroyed, would these voracious wolves overtake and devour the two celestial chariots.

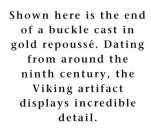

Shown here is the end of a buckle cast in gold repoussé. Dating from around the ninth century, the Viking artifact displays incredible detail.

THE CREATION OF MAN

One day, while walking along the edge of the sea checking their handiwork, Odin, Vili, and Ve came across two fallen trees. One was an elm tree, the other an ash. Odin imbued each tree with the spark of life. Vili endowed them with spirit and a thirst for knowledge. Ve granted them the gift of the five senses. When all was finished the two trees no longer resembled trees at all, but appeared to be smaller versions of the gods themselves. They were the first man and woman. The man had come from the ash and was named Ask. The woman had come from the elm and was named Embla. The sons of Bor granted these new beings the realm of Midgard.

THE CREATION OF THE DWARVES AND ELVES

The sons of Bor discovered that while they had been busy, Ymir's rotting flesh had produced a slew of creatures. These creatures were dark, smelly beasts. And, although repulsive, they did have life and therefore the Aesir felt an obligation to help them.

The gods assessed the foul, wriggling creatures and quickly changed them into forms fitting their natures. The creatures who were of an evil, greedy nature took on a hunched-over, gnarled shape. They were hearty, though, and could easily survive where others could not. These beings were called dwarves and were banished to a place called Svartalfheim, a subterranean world, far below the surface of Midgard. Here they would be able

to dig through the rich earth, uncovering the precious metals and gems they so treasured. They had to be careful never to venture to the surface during the day, for the slightest touch of a sunbeam on their bare skin would instantly turn them to stone.

The creatures who possessed a gentle, kind spirit, with no ill will or greed to taint their souls, were changed into beautiful beings, light as the air itself; these were the elves. They were told they could live in the land of Alfheim, "world of the white elves," which could be found between Asgard and Midgard. In Alfheim the elves had safe haven; and whenever they chose they were permitted to fly down to Midgard for whatever reason took

their fancy, be it to play with a flock of birds soaring through the air or to tend to some flowers that needed special care.

ASGARD AND THE AESIR

Seeing that everything was now fairly well taken care of, Odin, the ruler of the gods, ordered that a great meeting take place in the center of Asgard, the area the gods had set aside for themselves before they undertook the rest of creation. At this grand meeting the gods decided that within the realm of Asgard

warfare was not welcome. Peace would reign as long as the Aesir ruled. They then set up a magnificent metalworking shop, from which they fashioned their weapons and from which came the enormous and beautiful palaces and halls that would eventually fill Asgard.

Running through the center of it all was the great ash tree Yggdrasil, the mightiest tree ever. Its three roots, one in Jotunheim, one in Niflheim, and one in Asgard, gave the uni-

verse its stability. Near each of these roots flowed a spring. The root in Niflheim was near the mighty Hvergelmir. Here lived the evil serpent Nidhogg, who continually gnawed on the root of the mighty tree, hoping one day to bite clean through and thereby cause the universe to fall into chaos.

Near the root in Asgard flowed the well of Urd. Here was located Gladsheim, the meeting hall of the gods. The three Norns, the goddesses of destiny, whose names were Urd (past), Verdandi (present), and Skuld (future), lived near this spring, from where they controlled not only the destiny of man but of the universe as well.

The root in Jotunheim was near the spring of wisdom, which was guarded by Mimir. It was here that Heimdall, the watchman of the gods, kept the horn that would be blown at the beginning of Ragnarok. For countless eons the Aesir, giants, dwarves, elves, and man lived in harmony. Everyone kept out of everyone else's way and no trouble was caused. It was a golden age. But, like all good things, it was to come to an end.

THE WAR BETWEEN THE AESIR AND THE VANIR

There were some creatures that even the tolerant Aesir could not stand. One of them was a witch named Gullveig. Whenever she visited Asgard all she could talk about was her desire for gold and how much she loved the precious metal. Such greed was repulsive to the Aesir. On one of her visits her obnoxious rantings and unseemly gold-lust became too much for them to bear and they all rose up and killed her, throwing her body onto a large fire they'd built in the middle of Gladsheim.

But Gullveig's powers were mighty and she rose from the flames reborn. Three times the Aesir slew her and three times they set her body on the pyre but each time she rose from the flames as fresh as a newborn. After this the Aesir began calling her Heid, which means "shining one." Heid soon became the goddess of evil magic, letting loose her foul powers throughout the universe, tainting everything.

When the Vanir, the gods of the natural world, who lived in the realm of Vanaheim, not far from Asgard, learned of how the Aesir had played a part in the creation of this new black goddess, they became incensed. They declared war on the Aesir.

The battle raged furiously for eons, with neither side ever gaining much of an advantage. As soon as the Aesir delivered a crushing blow to the walls of Vanaheim, the Vanir would amass their magic and lay waste to the walls of Asgard. It eventually became obvious to both sides that there could be no winner in this war, and so a truce was called.

It was decided that the Aesir and the Vanir should live in peace. To cement this agreement the two sides agreed to exchange key leaders. The Aesir sent Vili and Mimir. Vili was widely thought of as a born leader, strong in both thought and action. Mimir, the guardian of the well of wisdom, was considered the embodiment of the well he protected. The Vanir sent Njord, the god of summer, and his son Frey, the god of sunshine and spring. Along with them came Kvasir, who was born from the combined saliva of Vanir and Aesir, and Freya, Frey's sister, who would become the goddess of beauty and love, as well as the queen of Odin's warrior maidens, the Valkyrs.

These gold brooches, which were found in Denmark, date from the tenth century. They were part of a Viking funeral cache.

The mysterious stonemason tries to restrain Svadilfari. Loki, in the guise of a beautiful mare, can be seen in the distance.

THE REBUILDING OF ASGARD'S WALL

Many years after the war with the Vanir the Aesir had yet to rebuild the protective wall around Asgard. Even for the gods it seemed too daunting a task. Yet they were all worried that by leaving their defenses down they were inviting an invasion by the frost giants.

One day Heimdall, the watchman of Asgard, came to Odin telling him of a stranger who had come demanding an audience with the Aesir. Odin called a meeting and soon all the Aesir were assembled in Gladsheim. The stranger entered the hall and offered to rebuild Asgard's wall. The gods were both excited and wary, since they knew there must be a considerable price for such a service. The stonemason said that he would rebuild the wall in a mere eighteen months, and that for payment he desired the hand of Freya, the goddess of love, as well as possession of the sun and the moon.

The gods were ready to run the craftsman out of Asgard right then, but Loki, the god of evil and trickery, spoke up, asking his fellow gods to at least consider the mason's offer. The stranger was led outside of Gladsheim so that the Aesir could discuss the situation.

Loki's plan was to agree to the mason's price, but to only allow the stranger six months, an impossibly short time, to finish the task. Loki figured that in six months the wall would be half-built and they wouldn't owe anything. The Aesir were hesitant to go along with Loki but couldn't find any fault with his plan, so they agreed.

When the Aesir's conditions were related to the mason, he agreed, but asked to be allowed the use of his horse, Svadilfari. At first Odin refused, but Loki convinced the king of the Aesir to agree to the stranger's demand.

The mason began work the next morning. Svadilfari proved to be more powerful than the gods had thought possible. The stallion was able to haul massive amounts of rock up to his master, who was then able to chisel them into shape and fit them into the wall almost as fast as Svadilfari could bring them.

As the end of the six-month period neared, the gods saw that all that was left to be built was the gateway, which would take no time at all to build. Anxiety filled the gods, most of all Freya, who hated even the thought of being married to the stonemason.

Odin called a meeting in Gladsheim where it was soon decided that since Loki had gotten them into the mess, Loki would have to get them out if he wanted to continue living in Asgard. With his quick words and quick mind, Loki devised a plan that he was sure would put the minds of the Aesir at ease.

That night Loki transformed himself into a beautiful mare and seduced Svadilfari. The shape changer led the fierce stallion far away from his master so that the next day the mason would have to haul the stones himself. With this added burden on his shoulders there was no way the mason could complete the job in time.

When the stranger found Svadilfari missing he knew he had somehow been tricked. In his anger he rushed into Gladsheim and voiced his complaint. His anger was so great that it became impossible for him to maintain his disguise and soon a lumbering, bellowing rock giant stood before the gods. Odin quickly called for Thor, the god of thunder, who killed the giant with one blow from his mighty hammer, Mjolnir.

Months passed and the Aesir soon completed the wall, but still no one knew what had become of Loki. Eventually Loki returned, crossing Bifrost (the rainbow bridge that led to Asgard) with an eight-legged colt in tow. Loki went to Odin and told him how he'd tricked Svadilfari into running away, and how he'd had to mate with the stallion in order to keep the beast from returning to the mason. The eight-legged colt was the offspring of that union. Loki gave the colt to Odin, telling him that it was, without question, the fastest horse in all the universe. The young horse was named Sleipnir and grew to become Odin's faithful steed. Asgard was now complete and secure once again. The Aesir, with Odin in command, began their rule.

This detail is from a ninth-century picture stone found on Gotland that probably served as part of a funerary tribute. Made of limestone, the picture stone highlights several figures from the Norse canon; this detail shows Odin astride Sleipnir. He is being welcomed to Valhala by a Valkyr (the figure to the left of Sleipnir).

ODIN—KING
OF THE AESIR

O f all the Norse gods, Odin was one of the most tragic and noble. He possessed a wisdom so vast and all-encompassing that he was unable to be of good cheer, since he was able to see forward into the future to the time of Ragnarok, when the gods and the universe would be destroyed. He is sometimes known as Wotan or Woden, and the day Wednesday is named after him. He was typically characterized as the spirit of the universe itself, the god of the wisdom that comes with age, and the protector of warriors whose hearts are

Odin, the one-eyed god, sits upon Hlidskialf (the foot of which depicts Yggdrasil and the Norns) observing the nine worlds. Clutching Gungnir, Odin is flanked by Hugin and Munin.

true and courageous. He was also thought to be somewhat connected with the few summer months of the north. During these short periods every year Odin was thought to rule. During the longer periods of winter Odin relinquished his rule to Uller, the god of winter.

Odin was one of the original gods, the sons of Bor, and therefore nearly all the other gods of Asgard are in some way descended from him; hence his other name, Allfather. Odin was the son of Bor and the giantess Bestla and is usually depicted as a distinguished old man with a wide-brimmed, floppy hat concealing his face in shadows. From Hlidskialf, his throne, he was able to view the entirety of the nine worlds and witness the goings-on of man and god alike. His second but most beloved wife, Frigga, was the only other being who was allowed to sit upon Hlidskialf.

Odin had two other wives besides Frigga. His first wife was named Jord, or Erda. She was the offspring of the Primordial Chaos surrounding Ginnungagap and an unknown giantess. With her Odin produced Thor, his mightiest child. His third wife was named Rinda. She represented the barren, cold earth of winter and only begrudgingly allowed Odin to be with her for a short time every year. During this time the land warmed and the brief northern summer occurred. With Rinda, Odin produced a son, Vali. Vali was one of the few gods to survive Ragnarok, and figured prominently in the story of the death of Balder, the god of light and truth.

Odin is usually shown holding his magnificent spear, Gungnir, and wearing the armband Draupnir, which self-replicated every seven days. Respectively, these objects symbolize Odin's strength and fer-

tility. Perched atop Odin's shoulder could be found the two ravens Hugin and Munin, their names meaning "thought" and "memory," respectively. They were Odin's far-reaching eyes and ears. Every day they left their lord, scouring the world for any news that the king of the Aesir might have overlooked.

Odin also had two wolves familiar to him, Geri and Freki. Symbolizing the innate hunting instinct of their master, these two wolves received every scrap of meat that was set before Odin. Odin himself refrained from eating, his only sustenance being the wonderful mead, or honey wine, that was served in Valhala, the hall of the chosen slain. When Odin found it essential to leave Asgard he rode his eight-legged horse Sleipnir, the offspring of Loki and Svadilfari. Sleipnir was the fastest horse in the nine worlds.

On Midgard Odin's furious spirit of battle was said to possess a certain type of warrior called a berserk. The name comes from the fact that these warriors wore bearskin shirts into battle instead of armor, believing that

mighty Odin would shield them from all harm. They fought in insane rages, slashing at anything that might come their way, including members of their own clan, or boulders and trees if nothing else was around. Their fearlessness and sheer brutality made them formidable enemies, and their undying ferocity endeared them to Odin.

MIMIR'S WELL — THE SOURCE OF ODIN'S WISDOM

Soon after Ymir had been vanquished and Odin and his brothers had constructed the world from the giant's corpse, Odin visited Mimir, the guardian of the well of wisdom. In the waters of the well one could supposedly see the future being played out.

Odin approached Mimir, pleading for a draught of the wondrous water, knowing full well that in order to fulfill his position as king of the gods he would need the magical wisdom the well could endow. Mimir agreed to Odin's wishes but on one condition: Odin must pluck out one of his eyes and leave it in the well. Odin readily complied, plucking out an eye and letting it sink to the bottom where it was still visible, a pale yet lustrous orb that became a symbol for the moon. His remaining eye therefore became symbolic of the sun.

With the water of the well flowing through his body Odin gained the wisdom he longed for. Returning from the well he tore a branch from Yggdrasil and from it fashioned his spear, Gungnir. It was not long before Odin realized the price that such wisdom exacts from its holders. He was able to see clearly the transitory nature of the universe and even the eventual fate of the gods at Ragnarok. He realized, in a fatalistic flash, that nothing was permanent, that everything would eventually

perish. The weight of this wisdom caused his normally cheerful face to sour; from that point on his countenance was that of a being who had seen his own doom. It is for this reason that Odin drank only mead and never ate. With the fate of the universe already clear to him, Odin required a great deal of solace (hence his strict diet of alcoholic beverages).

Geri and Freki, Odin's two wolf familiars, symbolized not only their master's innate cunning but his savagery as well.

THE FEAST OF THE EINHERIAR

Odin had three main palaces in Asgard: Gladsheim, the meeting hall of the gods; Valaskialf, where Hlidskialf stood; and Valhala, the palace of the chosen slain, which was situated in the middle of Glasir, a magnificent wood with trees that had leaves of red gold.

Valhala was the final resting place of those who had died with honor, in the fury of battle. To die in battle was the noblest death a Norseman could hope for. To die of old age or disease was considered a "straw" death, referring to the straw beds the infirm were placed on. Such a death was considered highly ignoble. In fact, most Norsemen preferred to fall on their own swords than face the indignity of a straw death.

When a battle raged in Midgard, Odin would dispatch his warrior maidens, the Valkyrs. These virgin demigoddesses would fly to earth on their steeds and select from the fray those warriors who had fallen with battle-lust in their eyes and blood on their hands. These chosen dead, or Einheriar, were then transported over Bifrost to Valhala.

Valhala was a palace of magnificent proportions. It was reported to have five hundred and forty doors, each one wide enough to allow eight hundred men passage at the same time. Highly polished spears lined the walls of the great hall, reflecting light from their tips, reminding the dead of the glory of battle. Long tables filled the room where the Einheriar would sit and feast with the king of the gods himself.

During the feasts the Valkyrs took on gentler roles. They served the warriors, making sure their plates were full of meat and their drinking horns full of mead. The meat was supplied by a divine boar, named Saehrimnir, who was slain every day by Andhrimnir, the cook. Miraculously, after every feast Saehrimnir would recombine, ready for the next feast. There was never a lack of food in Valhala.

After the warriors had gorged themselves they would call for their arms, proceed into Valhala's courtyard, and spend the rest of the day hacking each other to bits until the dinner horn sounded once again. The wounds they had received immediately healed and the combatants, like the best of friends, would slap each other on the back, laugh heartily, and sit down again for another mighty feast. From his seat at the head of the hall Odin watched over every feast, pleased that such noble warriors were able to enjoy each other's company both on the battlefield and at table.

One of the Valkyrs (Odin's select band of warrior maidens) summons a fallen warrior to the halls of Valhala.

CREATION OF RUNES

Of the many things Odin was credited with, the invention of runes is one of the most noteworthy. Realizing that only through pain and hardship is knowledge ever attained, Odin hanged himself from a branch of Yggdrasil for nine days and nights, staring into the inky blackness of Niflheim, contemplating his vast wisdom and the best manner to make that wisdom accessible to man and god alike. When he undertook this torturous labor, his body failed him and he died. Through sheer force of will he forced himself to be reborn with the knowledge known only to the dead intact inside his skull. From this knowledge he fashioned the runic symbols.

Their primary use was as objects of divination and fortune-telling. Later on people realized the value of the runes as symbols for record-keeping and decoration, especially on weapons. These runes became the characters in the earliest northern alphabets.

(TRANSLITERATION OF THE LEADEN TABLET.)

✝ (AT) Þ(E)R KUEN(E) SINE PRINSINED (B)AD (M)OTO LAN-
ANA KRISTI DONAVISTI GARDIAR IARDIAR
IBODIAR KRISTUS UINKIT KRISTUS REG-
NAT KRISTUS IMPERAT KRISTUS AB OMNI
MALO ME ASAM LIPERET KRUX KRISTI
SIT SUPER ME ASAM HIK ET UBIQUE
✝ KHORDA ✝ IN KHORDA ✝ KHORDAE
(t) (M)AGLA ✝ SANGUIS KRISTI SIGNET ME

RUNES, A. D. 1000.*

ABOVE: This ninth-century limestone tablet depicts some of the rather visceral pleasures to be enjoyed by the Einheriar in Valhala, where the feasting and fighting was endless.

LEFT: This tablet, which dates from around A.D. 1000, was discovered in Denmark in 1883. The first two lines of runes are in early Danish, and the remaining lines are in Latin.

FRIGGA—QUEEN
OF THE AESIR

Daughter of Odin and Jord, Frigga, the personification of the earth, went on to become her father's second, yet favorite, wife. Their marriage was a cause of great rejoicing throughout Asgard. Afterward, Frigga assumed the role of goddess of marital love and fidelity.

As her husband's eyes (the sun and moon) were always visible to those down in Midgard, it is only natural that the men of earth would associate the sovereignty of the sky with Frigga. A perfect queen, she surrounded the vision

---

Frigga, one of Odin's wives and Queen of the
Aesir, was believed to travel in a chariot
drawn by a pack of the most loyal creatures
in the annals of history, dogs.

RIGHT: In her role as chief attendant to the eminently vain Frigga, Fulla can be seen here handing jewelry to her queen.

BELOW, RIGHT: One of Frigga's duties was to spin the fabric of the clouds over Midgard.

of her husband. She alone had the honor of being able to sit alongside her husband on Hlidskialf, able to view the goings-on throughout the world. Like her husband, Frigga had an innate sense of the future, but whenever she was questioned about some future event her only response was a silent stare. Unlike her husband, Frigga felt that the future was something best left unknown. Although she too knew of the eventual coming of Ragnarok, it didn't seem to bother her. She was content with the time allotted to her.

Frigga's palace in Asgard was known as Fensalir. Within its walls she sat at her jewel-encrusted spinning wheel, spinning clouds to float above Midgard. Frigga's spinning wheel can be seen in the night sky as what is also known as the belt of the Greek constellation Orion.

While Valhala was the final resting place for many a noble warrior, Fensalir was the home for married couples who longed for each other's company after death. Frigga took special care to admit only those couples whose love was pure and without blemish. Within Fensalir's walls those truly in love would never be parted.

While Odin had his Valkyrs, Frigga had her own band of attendants and maidens. They had no collective name. Each of them had specific attributes and personalities that defined them. Frigga was often represented as a vain goddess, so it was only natural that she should have an aide for her dressing and primping. This attendant was named Fulla. She was Frigga's most beloved sister and was entrusted with the most valuable of the queen's treasures. She was also Frigga's chief advisor and companion, and thus never far from the queen's side. Fulla would eventually

become an agricultural goddess, her long blonde hair representing the fullness and beauty of ripened grain. In many depictions Fulla is shown wearing a band in her hair, symbolic of the band around a sheaf of grain.

Another of Frigga's maidens, second in importance only to Fulla, was Hlin. Hlin was the goddess of solace. She was the one who quieted the tears and cries of mourners. Frigga's messenger was named Gna. Gna was considered to be the wind itself, able to travel over land or sea with amazing swiftness. On Hofvarpnir, her steed, Gna served Frigga in much the same way that the ravens Hugin and Munin served Odin: she traveled throughout the nine worlds and reported what she had seen to her queen.

Two of Frigga's assistants, Lofn and Vjofn, were mainly concerned with the encouragement of young love. Lofn's job was to make it possible that those destined for each other should find each other without hindrance, while Vjofn's job was to thaw the cold heart of an unwilling lover and to smooth out the differences between quarreling married couples. Gefjon, another of Frigga's faithful handmaidens, had a job that was somewhat related to those of Lofn and Vjofn; it was Gefjon's duty to comfort those men and women who had died unmarried.

Syn was the guardian of Frigga's palace. It was her station to make sure that no unwelcome guests ever bothered the queen. On earth she was credited, along with the god Forsetti, with overseeing trials. Eira was the goddess of medicine. She made sure that any illness afflicting the queen would immediately be cured. On earth she was responsible for teaching mortal women the healing arts. She pointed out which herbs had medicinal qualities and the proper method of stitching wounds. Vara was the overseer of oaths. She kept her ears open for any broken promises, and severely punished offenders.

THE TRICKING
OF ODIN

Even though Odin was considered impossible to deceive, there was one Aesir who was sometimes able to throw the wool over his eyes. That Aesir was Frigga.

One day the pair were seated upon Hlidskialf, awaiting the start of a battle down below. The war was between the Vandals and the Winilers. The Winilers had made supplications to Frigga for aid in their upcoming battle, as the Vandals had to Odin. When Frigga asked her husband which side he was going to favor Odin deftly responded that he hadn't made up his mind yet. He told her he was going to take a nap and whichever side he saw first when he awoke would be the side he would favor. Since Odin's couch faced the Vandal camp it was obvious to Frigga that her husband had already decided. This was a situation she would not allow. While Odin was deep in slumber, Frigga took it upon herself to gently lift god and couch together and turn them around so that they faced the Winiler camp. She was careful not to wake him. When Odin awoke he realized he'd been tricked but, since it would go against his nature, he did not go back on his word.

Found in Denmark, this pre-Viking statue of Odin dates from sometime in the first century A.D.

THOR—GOD
OF THUNDER

Considered the strongest of all the Norse gods, Thor was well loved for his quick temper and his single-minded hatred of giants. He was generally thought to be the son of Odin and Jord, although he was thought by others to be the son of Odin and Frigga. Soon after he was born, the infant Thor demonstrated his amazing strength by playfully tossing about ten massive bales of bear pelts, causing the Aesir, who had assembled to celebrate the birth of the latest god, to gape in astonishment.

Thor was the strongest of the Norse gods. He is shown here holding his hammer, Mjolnir, and restraining his goats, Tanngniostr and Tanngrisnt.

On the rare occasion when Thor needed aid in traveling—for instance, from Midgard to Asgard— he called upon his goats.

While growing up Thor was prone to violent fits of rage. Given his incredible strength it was decided that he should go and live with Vingnir and Hlora, the keepers of lightning, until he reached an age when his temper didn't have so much control over him. After he came of age Thor was admitted back into Asgard to sit in one of the twelve seats of Gladsheim. He was given the palace of Bilskirnir, which was more spacious than even Valhala. Bilskirnir lay in the realm of Thrudheim, a suburb of Asgard. Within the walls of Thrudheim resided the souls of the slaves and peasants who had dutifully served the slain masters who now resided in Valhala. (Thor was not only the patron god of peasants and slaves; he was also associated with healthy crops and the weather.)

Thor was the only god not allowed to cross into Asgard via Bifrost. It was feared that his footsteps, which were thunder itself, would destroy the magnificent bridge. Therefore, when Thor went to Gladsheim he had to travel in a roundabout way, crossing the rivers Ormt and Kormt and the streams of Kerlaug.

Thor possessed three magical weapons, all of which were perfectly suited to the god of thunder. Mjolnir, his hammer, was so destructive it could level mountains with one blow. Thor often hurled Mjolnir at his enemies since it would always return to him, no matter how hard it was thrown. Even though Thor's strength was unmatched in all the world, he possessed Megingjord, a magic girdle that when worn doubled the thunder god's power. He also had a magic gauntlet that allowed him to catch Mjolnir without harm when the hammer returned to him.

As his feet were the thunderbolts themselves, Thor rarely needed aid when traveling, but when he did he relied on his trusty steeds. They were the goats Tanngniostr, meaning "cracker of teeth," and Tanngrisnt, meaning "gnasher of teeth." These two gigantic goats pulled Thor's chariot.

Throughout his existence Thor had two wives, with whom he produced two children each. His first wife was the giantess Iarnsaxa. She bore him Magni and Modi, their names meaning "strength" and "valor," respectively. These two children were special in that they were destined to survive Ragnarok and live on in the reborn world. Thor's second wife was named Sif. Sif had magnificent hair of gold, as long and as full as the bountiful grain of the field. With Sif, Thor had a son named Lorride and a daughter named Thrud. Thrud had the physical attributes of a giantess but the beauty of a goddess. Given that she was such a delectable prize it should be no surprise that soon she was widely courted. One suitor was a clever dwarf named Alvis.

THOR'S TEST OF ALVIS

As a race the dwarves had one major problem—they had to avoid the light of the sun lest they be turned immediately into stone. This being the case Alvis was only able to woo Thrud during the dark of night. This proved to be beneficial since Thor was usually deep in sleep when Alvis came to visit. The dwarf was sure, and rightly so, that Thor would not be at all pleased with their relationship.

The young lovers grew more and more fond of each other, and soon Alvis asked for Thrud's hand in marriage. The daughter of Thor was only too happy to oblige. As fate would have it, on the very night the two became engaged, Thor returned to Bilskirnir late and discovered the amorous duo in the throes of passion.

His mind ablaze with anger, Thor challenged the dwarf to a test of intelligence in order to prove Alvis' worth as a possible husband for his beloved daughter. Alvis readily agreed to the thunder god's test and was soon being questioned on all the known languages of the world. Alvis had no problem answering all of Thor's questions. The test continued late into the night.

When it became obvious that Thor had no more questions to put to the dwarf, Alvis called for the tests to end and reached for the hand of his beloved. Unfortunately the dwarf had underestimated the wrath and the cunning of Thor. In spending so much time answering the countless questions put to him, Alvis had forgotten to keep track of the time. He no sooner felt his hand touch that of his bride-to-be than he felt the first rays of the rising sun touch his skin. Alvis was immediately turned to stone, setting an example for any other being who fancied the idea of dallying with Thor's daughter.

THOR'S JOURNEY TO JOTUNHEIM

It was summer in Asgard and Thor couldn't keep his eyes away from the far-off land of Jotunheim, the realm of the giants. The thunder god was certain that the giants would soon try to attack the Aesir; consequently, he felt it was his duty to travel to Utgard, Jotunheim's main city, and rid the universe of a few of its enormous inhabitants.

When word of Thor's impending journey made its way around Asgard, Loki approached him, saying that in Jotunheim one would need sharp wits. Thor knew that Loki was the sharpest of the Aesir so he asked Loki to accompany him on his travels. Soon the Thunderer and the Trickster were on their way to the land of the giants.

That evening, while riding in Thor's chariot above Midgard, the two decided it was time to rest. The house they came to was run-down and dilapidated, and the surrounding farm was in no better shape. Loki didn't approve of Thor's choice of lodging, saying that the people inside would hardly be able to accommodate them, but Thor decided that whatever the people could not provide he would.

When the farmer and his family saw the two gods they became very anxious. They graciously gave the gods whatever amenities they could. They provided soft beds, a warm fire, and friendly company. But when it came to food all they could offer were some pitiful vegetables— they had no meat.

Keeping to his word, Thor went out to his chariot

Found in Denmark, this early Viking figurine of Thor is made of amber.

and slew Tanngniostr and Tanngrisnt. He brought the carcasses inside and told the family to eat their fill. Thor warned them not to break any of the bones, which had to be placed back inside the goats' skins after dinner so that he would be able to resurrect the animals the next morning.

Unable to curtail his devious nature, Loki convinced one of the farmer's children to break a thigh bone to get to the delicious marrow inside. The boy did, and placed the broken bone back in the skin. The next morning Thor brought his two goats back to life, only to find that one of them was now walking with a limp. It was obvious to everyone that

Thor's instructions had not been followed. In recompense for the slight, Thor took the farmer's children, Thialfi and Roskva, to be his servants on the journey.

The four of them soon reached the ocean that separated Midgard from Jotunheim. Walking along the beach they came across an abandoned boat. Soon, with Thor paddling the craft, they beached on Jotunheim's shore. Traveling inland they came to a curious hall in the middle of the forest. There was no door, no gate. One entire side of the hall was open. When they walked inside, they discovered that the hall was bigger than either Valhala or Bilskirnir. As they were all exhausted, they decided to make camp. In the middle of the night the four were awoken by a noise that sounded like the very fabric of the universe being ripped apart. It was louder and more violent than any earthquake. They were on the brink of leaving the hall when the noise stopped. Deciding that the hall provided more safety than the outdoors, they opted to wait out the night in a smaller hall they had found, off from the main room. Here, Thor figured, if they were attacked, they would have a better chance of defending themselves. All through the night, the travelers were shaken by a deep rumble that had the intensity of a hundred thunderstorms.

The next morning they discovered the cause of the terrible cacophony: a giant was asleep outside the hall, snoring loudly. Thor woke him, ready to hurl Mjolnir at him, but when the giant stood up Thor was so amazed at the being's size that instead he asked the giant his name. The giant said his name was Skrymir, and that he recognized both Thor and Loki. He was friendly enough and offered to show the travelers the way to Utgard. He then bent down and picked up his gloves. One of the gloves had been the mighty hall the travelers had camped in. The smaller hall they had found was the glove's thumb.

This relief carving is a fragment from a tenth-century cross found in the churchyard in Gosforth, England. It depicts a fishing trip taken by Thor and Hymir, a giant from whom Thor and Tyr later stole an enormous caldron during one of their trips to Jotunheim.

Later in the day Skrymir told the four that he needed a rest. He tossed Thor his knapsack, offering them the food inside. He then settled down to nap. As Loki and the children built a fire, Thor tried to undo the knots that sealed the bag. He tugged and pulled and tried as hard as he could to open the bag but couldn't get any of the knots to budge. Loki tried as well but met with the same result.

Angry that they had been the butt of Skrymir's joke, Thor climbed atop the snoozing giant and brought Mjolnir down squarely on Skrymir's forehead. Skrymir's only reaction was a lazy mumble, asking if a leaf had fallen on his head.

A puzzled Thor decided that the four of them might as well get some rest, too, but the giant's snoring was as loud as the night before. So for a second time Thor climbed atop Skrymir and let fly with Mjolnir, landing another blow directly in the middle of the giant's head. Skrymir's eyes lazily opened and asked Thor if an acorn had fallen on his head. Thor didn't answer. He simply returned to where the others were camped, puzzled as to why his hammer was failing him.

Before dawn the snoring had become so violent that the four were being shaken where they lay. It was an infuriated Thor who shot up and hurled Mjolnir directly at Skrymir's temple. The hammer sunk in up to the hilt and then returned to him. The giant woke, rubbed his eyes, and asked if anyone had seen a bird fly by, since he'd just felt some droppings fall on his head.

With that Skrymir rose and bid the four farewell. Before he left he pointed them toward Utgard and warned them that when they arrived at the palace of Utgard-Loki, the king of the giants, they should mind their tongues. Giants, he told them, have little tolerance for tiny people like themselves.

Eventually they came to the gates of Utgard. Squeezing through the bars, they

Here, the ultraviolent Thor prepares to brain Skrymir, despite the fact that the giant is clearly at a disadvantage.

soon found themselves in the hall of Utgard-Loki. Utgard-Loki was amused to see such small creatures in his great hall. He recognized Thor and directed a few pointed insults at the Thunderer. Thor took these disparaging remarks in stride, noticing that he was surrounded on all sides by giants clutching enormous weapons.

Utgard-Loki then said that no one was allowed to stay in his palace unless they were able to prove their mastery over some craft or occupation, and that the new visitors were no exception to that rule. Loki was the first to meet the challenge. The Trickster boasted that he could eat faster than anyone in the hall. Utgard-Loki chuckled at this remark, and decided to pit the god of cunning against a giant named Logi.

The two were positioned at opposite ends of a huge table, on which were piled vast amounts of meat. On Utgard-Loki's word, the two began to eat furiously. When time was called, Loki had eaten all the meat set before him, leaving only a pile of bones. Logi, on his side of the table, had left nothing. He had eaten both meat and bone and therefore was declared the winner.

Next to meet the challenge was Thialfi. He boasted that he could outrun anyone Utgard-Loki cared to match against him. The giant Hugi was chosen to compete against the young boy in a series of three races. Everyone adjourned outside the palace to a strip of open ground. There the two runners positioned themselves for the first race. At Utgard-Loki's word the runners sprinted from their points. Even though he ran akin to the wind, Thialfi was not fast enough to beat Hugi, who proved to be so quick that he was able to turn around and greet the young boy when the youth passed the finish line.

The second race ended no better than the first. Hugi beat Thialfi by almost three times the distance he had in the first race. The third race was even more of a failure. Hugi reached the finish line before Thialfi was even halfway done.

Utgard-Loki then turned to Thor and asked him what type of competition he would like to enter. Without hesitation the god of thunder challenged anyone in the palace to a drinking contest.

Utgard-Loki had a massive mead-filled horn brought out. He told Thor that among the giants most could drain the horn in one draught. Some of the weaker giants needed two drinks to do the job, but none was so weak as to need three sips.

Thor lifted the horn to his lips and took a massive draught. He thought he'd certainly drained the entire horn. But when he put it down he saw that the level of the mead had only gone down a little. On his second attempt the level was again slightly lower than before, but the horn was no where near empty. Thor's third attempt drained an enormous amount of liquid from the horn but still it was not drained when he put it down. Utgard-Loki chuckled to himself and asked the god of thunder if there was any other contest he would like to undertake. Thor boasted that he could meet any challenge the giant King set before him.

Utgard-Loki told him that many giants considered it a great challenge to lift his cat. Thor agreed to the challenge and as soon as he had a monstrous cat sprang from underneath Utgard-Loki's throne. Thor grasped the mighty feline tightly around the waist and tried to lift it to no avail. Its paws were still firmly planted on the floor. He then got underneath the cat and tried to push it off the floor using his legs. His muscles were stretched almost to their breaking point and yet only a single paw was raised above the floor.

Frustrated that he had failed at this test as well, Thor challenged Utgard-Loki to provide him with a suitable wrestling partner. The giant King said that most of his fellow giants would feel it beneath them to wrestle one so puny as Thor, but agreed to see if his elderly mother Elli would consent to the fight.

Elli came to the great hall and accepted Thor's challenge. Thor threw himself at the old hag but found that she was far stronger than he had ever imagined an elderly giant could be. He could barely get her to move one foot out of place. Finally, without warning Elli switched her center of gravity and threw Thor off balance, forcing the proud god down on one knee.

At this point Utgard-Loki called a halt to the contests as it was getting late. He had food and drink brought to the weary travelers as well as soft bedding. Soon the four were fast asleep. They woke the next morning to see a wonderful breakfast table in front of them with Utgard-Loki at the head. They feasted as well as they had the night before. Then Utgard-Loki led them outside the walls of Utgard where he turned in his tracks and faced the party with a look of utmost sincerity on his face. He told Thor that never again would the god of thunder be let inside Utgard's walls. Thor had expected this; considering how poorly he had fared in each and every contest, Thor felt he had disgraced himself. Then Utgard-Loki told Thor the real reason for his banishment.

It had been he, Utgard-Loki, who had disguised himself as Skrymir and led the travelers to Utgard. Skrymir's bag, which had proved impossible to open, had actually been sewn shut with iron wire. He pointed to a series of three deep valleys, each one deeper than the one before it, which were made when Thor had tried to brain Skrymir with Mjolnir. At this point Loki couldn't help but crack a smile at the giant king's inventiveness.

Utgard-Loki went on to explain that the being Loki had competed against in the eating contest was none other than wildfire, which indiscriminately eats everything in its path. The man Thialfi ran against was none other than pure thought, impossible to outrace. Thor's countenance turned a bit when he learned that the horn he had tried to drain had been connected to the ocean itself and that now the ocean was visibly lower than it had been. The cat he had tried to lift off the ground was in actuality none other than Jormungand, the child of Loki, the gigantic serpent that encircled Midgard. Finally, Elli, the apparent old hag, was in fact, old age herself. Utgard-Loki expressed to Thor his deepest admiration since never before had one been able to fend off old age as Thor had done the previous day.

When Thor realized he had actually frightened the giants with his various deeds, he swung Mjolnir high above his head, ready to brain Utgard-Loki for his deceptions. But when the hammer came down the king of the giants had vanished, as had Utgard itself. Thor's wrath was to have no outlet that day.

Soon Thor, Loki, Thialfi, and Roskva were on their return voyage. Thor reclaimed his chariot and goats from the farmer he had visited earlier, and soon was happily back in Thrudheim with the knowledge that the giants in Jotunheim were so terrified of him and his terrible power that they would never attempt to invade Asgard.

These three objects, which were found in Trendgaarden, Jutland, are (from left to right): an early cross; a mold for making crosses; and an amulet in the shape of Thor's hammer. Thor's hammer, a symbol of strength, was widely portrayed in Norse artifacts; of course, it is closely related to the cross, which was also widely portrayed in Iceland following the advent of Christianity there.

LOKI—GOD
OF LIES, CHAOS,
AND TRICKERY

O f all the Norse gods, Loki was the most unpleasant but also the most interesting. His personality swung from that of a malicious mastermind to a sly
yet good-natured troublemaker. Of all the gods Loki had the best-defined
yet the most ambiguous character. If that sounds like a contradiction, it is.
Contradiction was at the heart of Loki's personality. His chaotic nature and un-
bridled, indiscriminate impulsiveness are what made Loki the Trickster. He was
a deity possessed by the urge to create mischief. This urge occasionally got so

Pictured here half in light and half in darkness (an apt reflection of his chaotic nature) is
Loki, the Trickster. Above his right shoulder
is the giant Thiazi masquerading as an eagle.

strong that he forgot not only the safety of the other gods but his own as well. He was just as likely to unknowingly put himself in a bad situation because of one of his tricks as he was to imperil one of his fellow gods. For Loki the mere act of creating a disturbance was an end unto itself. He needed no grand reason for doing things, no great and glorious purpose. He only desired to stir up trouble and make existence problematic for whomever he came across. Sometimes his tricks were innocent and caused no damage. On other occasions they had disastrous effects. It is because of this randomness that Loki was primarily identified with the forces of chaos and discord. There was no rhyme or reason to his acts; there were only the acts themselves.

Some mythologists have proposed that Loki and Odin were, in fact, brothers, while others say that the Trickster was the son of the giants Laufey and Farbauti, and that Odin and Loki were brothers only in the sense that they, at one time, swore an oath of blood brotherhood, a common practice among the Norse. Regardless of his personal relationship to Allfather, Loki should be considered the ideological antithesis of Odin. Where Odin was good and wise, Loki was evil and thoughtless. Where Odin was noble, Loki was cowardly. Where Odin was prudent, Loki was careless. In the Norse canon these two gods represent the extreme ends of the moral spectrum. Loki is usually depicted as a handsome young man with a devilish demeanor. He is the very essence of life itself in all its chaotic glory. No conscience lies behind his eyes, no pity in his heart. He exists only for entropy's sake, and is found performing as many good as evil deeds.

One needs only to look at the myth of the building of Asgard's wall to see Loki at his most helpful. It is Loki's firm persistence that persuades Odin to hire the nomadic mason. Likewise, when he accompanies Thor to Jotunheim he is the first to accept Utgard-Loki's challenge. Earlier in the same story Loki coerces the young Thialfi to break open a leg bone of one of Thor's goats to get to the marrow, despite the direct orders of the Thunderer. On the surface this might appear to be malicious, given that Loki knew that Thor would demand retribution when he discovered the violation. As events unfolded, however, Loki's actions ended with Thor making Thialfi and his sister Roskva his attendants, the assistance of whom proved to be most helpful when they finally reached Jotunheim. In fact, if Loki hadn't played a particularly spiteful trick on Sif, Thor's wife, many of the Aesir's fabulous treasures would never have been made.

LOKI'S BARGAIN WITH THE DWARVES AND THE ORIGINS OF THE TREASURES OF THE AESIR

One night, while Sif was fast asleep, Loki stole into her bedroom and quietly cut off her magnificent golden hair. He let the tresses fall where they would and left, chuckling to himself for having played such a fine joke.

The next morning, Thor did not find the situation so amusing. He cornered the Trickster and throttled him. Fearing for his life, Loki agreed to travel to the realm of Svartalfheim, the land of the dwarves, and convince the sons of Ivaldi, the most talented craftsmen of all the dwarven race, to create another head of golden hair for Sif and to empower it with their magic so that it would grow like true hair when placed on her head.

This portion of a twelfth-century tapestry is from Halsingland, Sweden. From left to right, the figures are Odin, Thor, and Frey. Odin is shown holding an axe (instead of his spear Gungnir), Thor holds Mjolnir, and Frey holds an ear of corn.

Loki traveled to the dank recesses of Svartalfheim and found the brothers working furiously at their smithy. He begged them to make the golden wig. He also asked them to make gifts for both Odin and Frey as well, since they were almost as angry at him as was Thor, and therefore presents for them were a most politic consideration.

At first the dwarves were not interested in helping Loki, but when the Trickster told them that their work would bring about not only the gratitude of Odin, Frey, and Thor, but recognition of their skills as craftsmen throughout Asgard, the brothers were more than happy to begin. The dwarves set to work and soon hammered out Sif's golden wig. Their creation was finer and more luxurious than her real hair had ever been. For Frey, the god of sunshine and king of the elves, they built the ship Skidbladnir, which could be folded up and carried in a pocket. For Odin they made the terrible spear Gungnir, which

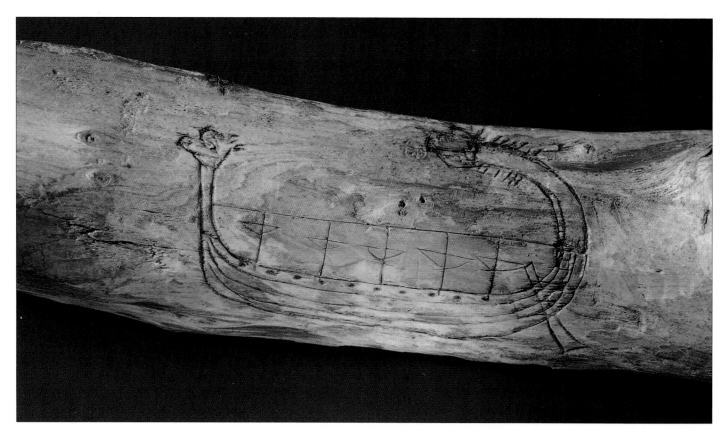

would become so revered a weapon that an oath sworn upon its blade could never be broken, by god or man. Pleased with the creations, Loki thanked the brothers and began his return trip to Asgard.

On the way to Asgard Loki came across two other dwarven brothers, Brokk and Eitri. The two expressed great interest in the treasures the Trickster was carrying, boasting that their skills at metallurgy far exceeded those of the sons of Ivaldi. Loki disagreed with the two and offered up a contest to test their skills. Loki bet his own head that the two wouldn't be able to fashion better gifts than the ones he now held. Brokk and Eitri jumped at the challenge, confident in their skills. Also, they thought, it would not be a bad thing to rid the world of Loki once and for all.

They sat Loki down in a comfortable chair in a luxurious room, with a full horn of mead, and retired to their smithy. With Brokk working the bellows and Eitri manning the hammer and anvil the two soon fashioned three magnificent items. They made the golden-haired boar Gullinbursti for Frey, which was capable of carrying its rider anywhere in the world, even into the darkness of the underworld, since its hair radiated a brilliant light by which to navigate. For Odin they made the arm ring Draupnir, which when worn would self-replicate. Their greatest accomplishment, though, was the hammer Mjolnir, which they made for Thor.

With these latest gifts now finished, Brokk and Loki set off for Asgard to place the treasures before Odin, Thor, and Frey, and have them decide which pair of craftsmen was the more talented.

The three gods were more than pleased with everything Loki had brought back, but agreed that of all the gifts there was none finer than Mjolnir, since it alone would be able to defend Asgard from the giants. Brokk cackled with glee when he heard the Aesir's decision. He immediately demanded that Loki make good on his bargain and relinquish his head.

Loki agreed that he had promised his head if he lost the wager, but reminded Brokk that their bet had said nothing about his neck, which would have to be cut through for Brokk to get his prize. Grudgingly Brokk relented. The Trickster had outthought his opponents. But then, having a glimmer of insight as to how the Trickster's mind worked, Brokk demanded that he be allowed to sew Loki's lips together, since technically he did now own Loki's head. No fault could be found with this and so, taking Eitri's finest awl in hand, Brokk carefully and tightly sewed Loki's lips together. If he couldn't kill the god, at least the dwarf could silence him.

After Brokk left Asgard to return home Loki ripped the stitching out. The voice of the Trickster was free once again and the fabulous weapons and treasures of the gods had been made, all because of Loki's practical joke. But just as Loki could be unintentionally helpful he could just as easily cause massive amounts of damage and mayhem without any malice aforethought.

LOKI AND ANGRBODA

Loki often took trips to Jotunheim to visit the giantess Angrboda. With her he produced three of the world's most hideous monsters. The oldest of the three was Fenris the wolf, a monster so terrible that only Tyr, the god of war, was able to imprison it. The middle child was Jormungand, the serpent that encircled Midgard, lying at the depths of its oceans. Their last child was Hel, who became the goddess of the underworld, the resting place of those who died of illness or old age. Hel was depicted as fairly normal-looking from the waist up, but hideously decayed and rotting from the waist down. She fed on the corpses of those who had died straw deaths; hence her realm was filled with the stench of decay.

Loki's most despicable act, the one that caused him to be banished from Asgard alto-

This soapstone artifact from the late Viking period was found on a beach in Denmark. Incised on the stone is Loki's face; note that the Trickster's lips are here sewn shut.

gether, was his persuasion of Hodur, the god of winter, to throw a spear made of mistletoe at his brother Balder, the god of light, causing the beloved Balder to die. By doing this Loki forever incurred the wrath of all the Aesir. The Trickster was thrown out of Asgard and told never to return.

Banishment didn't stop Loki, though. He returned once while the gods were having a massive banquet in Gladsheim. He strode into the hall and started shouting obscenities at the top of his lungs. His descriptions were of such a vulgar nature that the feasting gods were momentarily put off their food. After that he began insulting each of them in detail, listing their various problems and creating many more out of his own imagination. When he came to Sif, however, he had the misfortune to pontificate too loudly just as Thor, who had been absent until then, walked up behind the Trickster in Gladsheim's entranceway. Outraged that Loki was insulting his wife in such a crude manner, Thor bellowed with rage and began swinging Mjolnir around his head faster than the eye could follow. Realizing that he'd outstayed his rather flimsy welcome, Loki dashed off, not wanting to be on the receiving end of Thor's devastating weapon.

Loki's respite was brief. The Aesir were now infuriated with Loki, and Odin himself decreed that the Trickster should be captured and punished for his deeds.

LOKI'S FINAL
CAPTURE AND
TORTURE

Knowing he was being hunted, Loki built a square hut on top of a hill. Each of the four walls had a door that Loki always kept open. By doing this he hoped he would always be able to tell when someone, especially Thor, was approaching.

Down the hill from this hut ran a stream, which, if he was ever cornered, would serve as Loki's escape route. He planned to transform himself into a salmon, throw himself into the rushing waters, and avoid whatever punishment the gods might want to inflict upon him. Learning that Loki had made such provisions, Thor decided to have a magnificent net fashioned that he would throw across the stream when the salmon-Loki was swimming down its current. With net in hand, Thor, Odin, and Kvasir, the ancient god of inspiration, tracked Loki to his lair and soon netted the mischievous god.

With Balder's killer now in their custody, the Aesir began to devise an appropriate punishment. They decided Loki would be tortured in Midgard, since Asgard had, with Balder's death, seen enough blood. Before traveling there, they tracked down two of Loki's children, his sons Vali and Narvi. Vali was changed into a wolf and thrown into a mad rage. He attacked his brother, ripping out his entrails, and then ran off, mouth foaming, towards Jotunheim.

Using Narvi's intestines as binding, the Aesir tied Loki down to three massive rocks. A hideous serpent was then positioned above Loki's face so that its venom would drip down, unrelentingly, into his eyes. Sigyn, Loki's wife, stood faithfully by her husband's side, catching the majority of the terrible venom in a bowl. But when the bowl became full she had to leave her post and empty it, leaving Loki's face momentarily vulnerable to the fiery venom.

This was to be the fate of the god of lies— to have his face continuously burned until the time of Ragnarok. During this time Loki's anger and hatred towards the rest of the Aesir grew a thousandfold.

Here, the loyal Sigyn catches the serpent's venom before it can reach Loki's face. Note Loki's bindings, which were made from the innards of his son Narvi.

TYR—GOD
OF WAR

Tyr was the son of Odin and Frigga, or by some accounts of Odin and an unnamed giantess who personified the oceans. The bravest of the Aesir, Tyr was the god of battle and martial honor. Thus it was Tyr, along with Odin, whose name was invoked before battles.

Tyr was no god of blind battle rage, though. He was the god of honorable battle, of strategy and cunning. He was such a respected god that Tuesday, or "Tyr's day," was named in his honor.

The noble Tyr was the personification of the honorable warrior; his trustiworthiness was such that it cost him his hand.

He is usually depicted as a well-built, muscular god with only one hand. In this hand could always be found his sword, which he never let out of his sight. He was the patron god of swords, and his name was inscribed on many Norse blades.

It is unclear if Tyr had his own palace in Asgard, as no mention of one is ever made in the texts available today. Whether he had one or not, the other gods were always more than ready to accommodate him as a guest. The episode Tyr figures the most prominently in is that of the binding of Fenris, the monstrous wolf-child of Loki.

One of the hideous brood that Loki produced with Angrboda, Hel fed on the corpses of the ignoble. She was herself more corpse than flesh from the waist down.

THE BINDING OF FENRIS

Soon after Loki and Angrboda produced Fenris, Jormungand, and Hel, the Aesir learned of the monsters' existence. These were three of the most frightening creatures that had ever lived in the universe, and therefore it was not without cause that Odin questioned the Norns, the three goddesses of fate, as to what to do. They told Odin that all three creatures were the living embodiments of evil and should be dealt with as soon as possible to avoid any trouble they might cause.

At Odin's command a group of Aesir sneaked into Jotunheim one night and overpowered Angrboda. With the giantess incapacitated the Aesir kidnapped her three children and brought them back to Asgard, where the gods hoped they could figure out what to do with the atrocities.

Odin quickly banished Hel to Niflheim, where she would live out her days as the goddess of those who died natural, and therefore dishonorable, deaths. The dark realm of Niflheim suited Hel very nicely. She was a particularly hideous being, her lower half decayed and rotting. In her kingdom she feasted on the corpses that were sent to her, cracking their bones and licking out the marrow with her tongue. Her appetite for such delicacies was never sated.

Jormungand, the serpent, was thrown by Odin into the circle of ocean that surrounded Midgard. The snake quickly sank to the bottom, where he lived on, growing so long that eventually his head met his own tail, completely encircling Midgard.

When it came to Fenris, Odin was hesitant to banish him. He seemed like an ordinary wolf in every respect, and since Odin was fond of wolves he granted the young Fenris free reign over the fields and woods of Asgard.

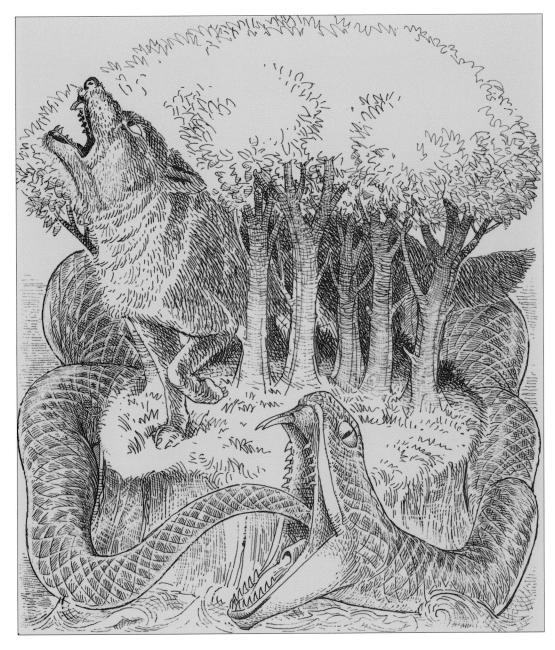

This soon proved to be a problem, since Fenris' growing hunger caused him to bellow and howl, disturbing all the Aesir. Tyr took it upon himself to regularly track down the wolf and feed him huge haunches of meat to quiet him. Because of these feedings, Tyr was the only Aesir that Fenris even remotely trusted.

One day Odin noticed that Fenris was growing noticeably larger with every passing day. He then remembered the Norns' prophecies, especially the one in which they had foretold that Fenris would eventually slay him. Odin knew it was impossible to change what the Norns had foreseen, but at the same time he didn't want to hasten his demise. He ordered that Fenris not be killed but instead bound tightly.

The first binding implement they employed was called Laeding, a massive iron chain that intimidated even Thor. They approached Fenris and asked him if he would consent to be bound. After carefully sniffing the chain and trying it between his teeth, Fenris allowed the gods to bind him with it. The Aesir tied Laeding around the wolf, but as soon as they were finished, Fenris stretched his muscular body and popped the iron links apart as if they were paper.

The mighty Odin, here depicted with both eyes, takes stock of the nine worlds as Hugin and Munin, his raven familiars, bring him news of the doings of god and human alike.

The Aesir tried a second time to immobilize Fenris, this time using an enormous chain called Dromi. It was twice the strength of Laeding, with links so large that no one on Midgard would have been able to move even one. The chain was secured around Fenris, but, as with Laeding, the wolf broke Dromi with relative ease.

Odin realized that drastic measures were going to have to be employed. He sent Skirnir, Frey's messenger, to Svartalfheim to convince the dwarves to create an unbreakable fetter for the terrible wolf. Only after being promised unbelievable amounts of gold did the dwarves consent to make the item. Into its making went six ingredients that only the magic of the dwarves could isolate—the sound of a moving cat, the beard of a woman, the roots of mountains, the voices of fish, the sinews of bears, and the spit of birds. All of these things, invisible to the eye and impossible to find, went into the construction of the magical ribbon Gleipnir.

Skirnir returned to Asgard, Gleipnir in hand. The gods once again set out to find Fenris and convince him to let them tie him up. The wolf took one look at Gleipnir and immediately suspected a trick. The ribbon was so thin it seemed it would snap in a light wind. With a vicious growl Fenris made it clear that he would not allow himself to be bound with the obviously magical ribbon. The gods then tried to bargain with him, telling him that if he was unable to break free of Gleipnir they would release him. Fenris did not believe the gods in the slightest and another fierce growl convinced them to keep their distance. Seeing as how this situation was going nowhere, Tyr alone approached the wolf and offered up a gesture of faith that he hoped would change Fenris' mind. If Fenris consented to be bound by Gleipnir, Tyr would place his hand in Fenris' mouth to ensure that the word of the gods would be kept when it

came time to untie him. Hesitantly Fenris agreed. If anyone else besides Tyr had put forth the proposition he would have bitten them in two, but he remembered the god who had been kind enough to feed him when he was a hungry pup.

Tyr placed one of his hands between Fenris' dripping jaws as the Aesir wound Gleipnir round and round the massive wolf. After they had finished, Fenris tried to move and found it impossible. The fur on his back bristled with anger and he demanded to be let free. When none of the Aesir made the slightest move to free the wolf, Fenris clamped down his jaws, biting off Tyr's hand.

Fenris remained bound by the magical ribbon until the time of Ragnarok, when Gleipnir succumbed to the evil in the air and limply fell to the earth. Fenris then took his revenge on Odin, the god who had suggested the wolf be bound in the first place. On the battlefield of Vigrid the enraged wolf devoured mighty Odin in one massive gulp.

Here, Odin and company bind Fenris with Gleipnir, the remarkably strong dwarvish ribbon. Tyr, on the right, has just lost his hand.

FREY—GOD
OF SUNSHINE
AND THE ELVES

Frey was the son of Njord, the god of the winds and seas, and Skadi, daughter of the storm giant Tjasse. Frey, who came to Asgard with his father and sister, was of Vanir descent. Frey was the god of good weather and sunshine—things invaluable to the beleaguered Norsemen, who spent a good deal of the year in dusky blackness and freezing cold. Because of his life-giving nature, Frey was held in high regard. Hence it was natural that Frey was depicted as a very handsome god.

Frey and Gerd travel over Midgard, led by
Gullinbursti, the magical golden boar.

After the war between the Aesir and Vanir, Frey was granted a seat in Gladsheim and given rule over the realm of Alfheim, the land of elves and fairies. This was a suitable kingdom for the lord of sunshine.

Frey also possessed the most feared weapon (with the exception of Mjolnir) in all the universe. When he was accepted into Asgard the gods furnished him with a sword that, when unsheathed, would fight an opponent under its own power.

Frey's trusty steed was the golden boar, Gullinbursti. On occasion Frey was known to travel in his magnificent ship Skidbladnir, which when not in use could be conveniently folded up and kept in his pocket.

As Frey was the god of sunshine, it is significant that his most prominent myth deals with his courtship of Gerd, the daughter of the frost giant Gymir. This myth is symbolic of the brief merging of frozen earth with nourishing sunlight that constituted the fertile, short-lived summer season the Norsemen so depended on.

This eleventh-century Swedish figurine represents Frey. Frey was considered among other things to be the god of fertility (note the phallus).

FREY'S COURTING OF GERD

One day while Odin was otherwise disposed Frey climbed atop Hlidskialf. If Odin had known of this Frey's punishment would have been quick and harsh, but Allfather was nowhere to be seen; hence Frey had no qualms about sitting in the seat from which all was visible. It was only a few moments until he spied, deep in Jotunheim, a lovely giantess emerge from her father's castle. Her name was Gerd, and Frey found it impossible to take his eyes off her. She was surrounded by an ice haze that enhanced and magnified her beauty. From that moment Frey knew that he must have the gorgeous giantess, but had no idea how to go about courting her since such involvement with the giants would be severely frowned upon in Asgard.

The constant ache of unrequited love began to take its toll on Frey. He ate less and less and barely touched his mead. Soon his father Njord took Skirnir, Frey's assistant, into his confidence. He asked Skirnir to find out what was troubling his son and take whatever measures were necessary to remedy the situation. Frey told his trusted aide of his desire for Gerd and his frustration at the fact that a relationship between them would never be allowed, by Aesir and giants alike.

Then inspiration hit Frey. He told Skirnir to travel to Jotunheim and tell Gerd of the god's love, in return for which Frey would grant Skirnir whatever treasures he had at his disposal. Skirnir agreed to go, requesting Frey's sword as payment for the service. He also asked the use of Frey's magical horse, Blodughofi, who was able to see clearly in the dark and was unafraid of flame.

Although hesitant to part with his fabulous sword, Frey couldn't resist the possibility Skirnir was offering. He accepted his friend's terms and for a moment was filled with joy, thinking only of Gerd's wondrous countenance. But he soon fell back into despondency, slumping in his throne and sighing heavily. Meanwhile, Frey's sword at his side, Skirnir mounted Blodughofi and headed towards Jotunheim.

Riding full speed Skirnir soon approached Gymir's castle. The closer he got the more clearly he heard the howling of Gymir's guard dogs, which were the fierce winds of winter itself. Up in the distance he saw the flaming circle that enveloped the castle, but since Skirnir knew Frey's steed was unafraid of flame, he transport her to the edge of the world, where her only view would be that of the gates of Niflheim. There she would grow so old and haggard that no man, giant, or god would ever want anything to do with her, save for the giant Hrimgrimnir, who lived near Niflheim. Hrimgrimnir was the vilest of the frost giants. His caresses would be like death itself.

After hearing Skirnir's threat and realizing that he indeed had the power to follow through on it, Gerd realized she had no choice but to accept Frey. Skirnir was delighted to hear Gerd's decision and was all set to ride back to Alfheim when she stopped him. She told him that she would meet with Frey in the forest of Barri after nine nights, claiming that she needed the time to prepare herself mentally for the change her life was going to take. After their woodland meeting, she would consent to be his wife.

Upon his return Skirnir told Frey the good news, but Frey did not see it as such. He wailed and howled in despair, complaining that nine nights was too long for his desire to go unfulfilled. As he had no choice, however, he resigned himself to wait. And, after the nine days had passed, the two met in the forest of Barri and consummated their relationship, making the barren forest sprout to life with the merging of cold, wintry earth and brazen, life-giving sunlight.

dug his heels into the horse's sides and plunged headfirst through the blazing barrier.

Luckily Skirnir arrived during a time when Gymir was out hunting. The messenger located Gerd with little difficulty and told her of Frey's great love for her. Gerd responded with indifference. She wanted nothing to do with a god whose occupation dealt with the warming of the land—she was a frost giant and had her loyalties. So fierce was her rejection of Frey that Skirnir became overcome with rage. He brandished Frey's mighty sword above his head and warned the giantess of what might befall her if she continued to refuse the affections of one so powerful.

Still the giantess rebuffed Frey. As a last resort Skirnir pulled out his own staff, which was covered in runes. With it, he told her, he would be able to make her into the loneliest person in the universe. He threatened to

LEFT: After their night in the forest of Barri, Frey led Gerd to her new home in Alfheim in a carriage drawn by his trusty boar, Gullinbursti.

BELOW: These three gold foils, from amulets used in ancient Norse fertility rites, are embossed with the images of Frey and Gerd coupling.

FREYA—GODDESS OF LOVE

reya was the Norse goddess of fertility and physical love. Whereas Odin's wife, Frigga, oversaw the marital side of love, Freya's job was to make sure the reproductive urge never died. She was the sister of Frey and the daughter of Njord, and, like her relatives, was of Vanir descent. After the war of the Aesir and Vanir, she, along with her brother and father, agreed to live in the realm of the Aesir as a peace offering. Among the goddesses Freya was by far the most beautiful. Her hair was more lovely than Sif's, her features more

---

This is a romantic depiction of Freya, Frey's sister, the Norse goddess of fertility and physical love.

Freya spies the dwarves forging Brisingamen. In return for the magnificent necklace, the underworld creatures demanded sexual favors from the goddess of love.

handsome than Frigga's. Despite her attractive countenance, however, the other goddesses held little jealousy toward her. As she was the goddess of physical love, her palace, called Sessrymnir, which was found in the realm of Folkvang in Asgard, was home to the wives and concubines of the Einheriar.

Since Freya had close relations with the chosen dead, it was only natural that Odin would choose her to become the leader of his elite force of warrior maidens, the Valkyrs. Some might think that being the queen of the battle maidens might compromise Freya's position as goddess of love, but one must remember that the Norse were a hearty race who found strength and physical prowess to go hand in hand with beauty.

As Valfreya, as she was known when leading the Valkyrs, Freya led her maidens down to the fields of battle, and by herself chose half of the slain who would be transported across Bifrost, the rainbow bridge, into Valhala. Because of this duty Freya is often represented as being dressed in battle armor: corselet, shield, helmet, and spear. Other depictions of her show her as being garbed in

the most feminine of flowing robes and dresses. Each personification is quite fitting to her character.

Freya was the proud owner of two fantastic objects, the necklace Brisingamen and her cloak of falcon feathers. Once, while she was visiting the land of the dwarves, Freya spied a number of the little people creating the most wonderful necklace she had ever seen. Her vanity was as elevated as her libido, and she immediately coveted the object. She pleaded with the dwarves for it, but they steadfastly refused it to her unless she would offer herself to them as payment. With a grimace, Freya accepted their proposal and, after an unpleasant few minutes, was the owner of Brisingamen, which would come to represent either the stars in the night sky or the undying fertility of the earth, depending on the version.

Freya's falcon cloak had the power to give its wearer the ability to fly. On a number of occasions Loki borrowed this magnificent object to help him out of whatever trouble he had gotten himself into at the time. Since she was such a beloved goddess the Norse dedicated a day of the week to Freya. Freya's day, or "Friday," is still held in great regard throughout the civilized world.

THE RELATIONSHIP OF FREYA AND ODUR

In some areas of the world, Freya was considered not only the goddess of love but the goddess of the fertile earth as well. Given this it is only natural that she would become attracted to Odur, who, like her brother Frey, was a personification of the nourishing sun. In some parts of the northern world he was also considered to represent the intoxicating power of pure love. In this respect it makes sense that he should be aligned with Freya.

Soon after they met they had two daughters, named Gersemi and Hnoss, who were so beautiful that the people of Midgard soon took to using their names as synonyms for anything lovely. For a while this family of four was quite content to live in Asgard, lazily whiling away the days, content with each other's company.

Then, as the summer sun is known to do, Odur began to wander throughout the world, looking for adventure. When Freya discovered that her husband was missing she broke down and began to weep, her tears falling to the earth. So warm and passionate were these tears that they soaked deep into the very rock of the earth, where they were transformed into gold.

After searching throughout Asgard and not finding her husband anywhere, Freya resigned herself to a long journey. She gathered up her falcon cloak, left Asgard, and began to scour the world, intent on finding her beloved husband. Along the way she flew over every known land and even some unknown lands, leaving behind her a trail of golden tears. It is for this reason that gold is to be found throughout every corner of the earth.

After a long and arduous search, Freya eventually found her wandering husband in the southern lands. She found him leaning against a myrtle tree, lazily relaxing in the daylight. She crept up behind him and fashioned a wreath out of the myrtle's flowering branches and placed it upon her head. She then emerged from her hiding place looking as lovely as the day they were wed. (For this reason it was customary among the Norse for brides to wear wreaths of myrtle.)

Freya asked no questions and held no grudges about what Odur might have been up to during his absence—she was simply

pleased to have him once again by her side. For his part Odur was more than happy to see his wife again since on his many travels he had never come across one so enchanting and lovely as Freya. Hand in hand, they took their own sweet time traveling back to Asgard, lingering in whatever land they happened to fancy at the time. As they went, the forces of nature celebrated Freya's return to happiness by creating the magnificent flowers and vegetation of summer in the couple's wake.

BRAGI—GOD OF POETRY AND IDUN—GODDESS OF YOUTH

The Norse god of poetry and music was named Bragi. He was the son of Odin and the giantess Gunlod. Not surprisingly, he was the prime deity of the scalds, the bards and poets who preserved the many tales of the Aesir in the compositions and poems that were later collected by the likes of Sturluson. Bragi is usually depicted as an old man cradling a golden harp in his arms. His grey hair and his long beard are typically seen flowing around his body, mimicking the waves of music and song that he personifies.

Bragi explains some musical point to his wife, Idun. She is balancing a bowl of the apples of immortality, which kept the Aesir young and vital.

Idun was generally considered to have had no parents. Being the goddess of eternal youth it is only natural that she should never have been born. It was also believed that Idun would never taste the sharp sting of death. Idun's main function in the Norse pantheon was to supply the wondrous golden apples of youth to the Aesir. She would supply the gods with these from time to time, making sure that old age never worked its way into either the minds or bodies of the Aesir. Such magical fruits were highly prized by the gods and also highly envied by the dwarves and giants, as will be seen.

BRAGI'S ORIGIN

After the war between the Aesir and the Vanir the two races cemented their truce by collectively spitting into a large jar. From this mass collection of spittle was created a god named Kvasir, a gentle deity who held within his blood all the knowledge and wisdom of the nine worlds.

Whenever he was approached with a simple query, Kvasir would answer it directly. If, for example, a farmer asked him if this year's harvest would be bountiful, Kvasir would answer the man truthfully and without hesitation. If someone came to Kvasir asking him for insight to a matter whose outcome was not black-and-white, Kvasir would answer the question with a question. By doing this Kvasir demonstrated that most people are able to answer their own questions.

It was not long before stories of Kvasir's wisdom reached the ears of two evil dwarven brothers, Fjalar and Galar. Like most dwarves, when these two heard of something extremely valuable, such as Kvasir's wisdom, they were overcome with a strong desire to possess it. Their minds plotting and planning, they invited Kvasir to dinner.

Never being one to refuse an invitation to a good dinner, Kvasir was soon dining under the earth in the company of the two brothers. To test Kvasir's knowledge they asked him about many things, all having to do with the petty squabbles and tiffs dwarves were constantly engaged in. Kvasir answered all their questions and they were soon convinced that his great wisdom must be theirs.

After dinner the brothers took Kvasir into an adjacent room for after-dinner drinks and conversation. The unwitting Kvasir was more than happy to accept their generosity. Their hospitality soon turned into treachery, though, for as soon as Kvasir set foot inside their study, the brothers unsheathed their concealed daggers and attacked the god of wisdom, stabbing him to death. From the wounds flowed Kvasir's blood, which was rich with his wisdom. Fjalar and Galar eagerly caught the flowing blood in three vessels: two jars called Bodn and Son, and a massive kettle called Odrorir.

The two greedy brothers then combined Kvasir's blood with rich honey, creating a wonderful mead that embodied the very soul of Kvasir's wisdom. It was a magical drink that would imbue anyone who tasted it with the gift of wisdom and the poetry that springs from such wisdom.

Soon afterwards Fjalar and Galar were host to the giant Gilling and his wife. The four sat down to dinner, starting up a conversation typical to the likes of dwarves and giants—all about property, greed, and who was the worst cheater in the universe. After dinner, Fjalar and Galar decided that Gilling should meet with an unpleasant end, since his words at the table had been less than pleasing to their ears. Suggesting an after-dinner sail, the two dwarves rowed Gilling far out into the ocean and purposely ran the boat into a large rock, sinking boat and giant together (Gilling couldn't swim). When the two brothers returned to their cave, they were greeted by the mournful wails of Gilling's wife, who knew

her beloved husband was dead. Fjalar and Galar quickly smashed her head in with a huge millstone, effectively quieting her high-pitched cries. It didn't take long for Gilling's son, the giant Suttung, to learn of his parents' deaths. He left Jotunheim for Svardalfheim, determined to find and bring to justice his parents' slayers.

Suttung quickly deduced who the murderers were. Grabbing the brothers by their necks he strode out far into the ocean with the intention of leaving the two to drown, just as they had done to his father. When their fate became clear the two evil brothers pleaded with Suttung, promising him their greatest treasure if he would just spare their lives. That treasure was, of course, the mead of Kvasir. Suttung accepted this offer.

Unlike the two dwarves, Suttung was not secretive about his possession of the mead, and soon word of its existence reached the ears of Odin, who was immediately disturbed that a giant should have so lofty a treasure. Disguising himself as a giant and adopting the name Bolverk, Odin left for Jotunheim determined to retrieve the mead of poetry, which he had learned was kept deep in the center of Hnitbjorg, Suttung's mountain palace.

He soon came to a field in Jotunheim where nine men were working in the employ of Braugi, Suttung's brother. They were harvesting a field and not having too good a time of it as their scythes were growing duller with each sweep, making the cutting very difficult. Odin approached the men and offered to sharpen their dull scythes with the whetstone he was carrying under his cloak. Soon all nine scythes were as sharp as razors and slicing through the long grain like hot knives through butter. The men, overjoyed with their newly sharpened tools, asked Bolverk if they could buy the whetstone from him. Odin replied that he would only sell the stone to the man who fed him in the grand manner he was accustomed to. As Odin never ate, this proposal was simply a ruse to uncover the true natures of the men.

Immediately Odin was besieged with invitations to dinner, each man trying to outdo the others in the size and selection of the supposed menus. Allfather recognized the greed in the men's eyes and, instead of accepting any of the offers, threw the whetstone high into the air. The men, all wanting to be the one to catch the stone when it returned to earth, scurried around, vying for the best position. In their hurried scuttle they ended up slicing open each other's throats with their scythes. Odin smiled, realizing that these deaths could easily be used to his advantage. He tucked the whetstone back into his cloak and began walking in the direction of Braugi's palace. When he arrived he found the giant sulking. Odin introduced himself as Bolverk and asked Braugi what the trouble was.

Braugi told the stranger that that very day all nine of his field hands had been killed, and now it would be near impossible to complete the harvest in time. Seizing the opportunity Odin volunteered to harvest the entire field, saying that he easily had the strength of nine men. When Braugi asked what type of payment he would require for such a service, Bolverk demanded a draught of Suttung's treasured mead as his salary.

Braugi reluctantly agreed to the terms, doubting if this lone man would be able to complete all the harvesting in one single summer. The season came and went and at its end the field stood bare, completely harvested by

Bolverk. Keeping true to his bargain, Braugi took the stranger to Hnitbjorg, Suttung's palace, where he asked his brother for the payment Bolverk required. Suttung scoffed at his brother's request, unwilling to part with even a drop of the mead.

Hearing this, Odin decided to it was time for trickery to come into play. When he and Braugi were outside Hnitbjorg, he took an auger from his belt and told Braugi that with it he would be able to drill a hole straight through Suttung's mountain palace.

Not believing Bolverk, Braugi grasped the auger and pressed it into the side of the mountain and began turning. The sound of the tool slowly grinding into the depths of the mountain made Odin's teeth rattle but the god didn't complain, knowing full well that the gullible giant would succeed in boring all the way through.

As soon as Braugi withdrew the drill and inspected the hole he had made, which did go completely through the mountain, Odin changed himself into a snake and slithered down the tube until he came to the room in the center of the mountain where Gunlod, Suttung's daughter, kept guard over the three vessels containing the mead of Kvasir.

When Allfather appeared in the chamber he turned back into the form of Bolverk, surprising the lonely giantess. Gunlod was soon overtaken with desire and the two of them lay together for three days. After this time Gunlod was so in love with the disguised Odin that she showed him where the three containers of mead were kept.

In three hearty draughts Odin emptied Odrorir, Bodn, and Son, holding the liquid in his mouth. He then changed into an eagle and flew out of the mountain and back to Asgard, spilling a small amount of the precious liquid in Midgard. This small amount became the inspiration for poets and bards all over the northern lands.

These tenth-century Viking coins, featuring an unidentified hero, were found in England.

Back inside Hnitbjorg, Gunlod couldn't restrain her tears. The man she had fallen in love with had fled after betraying her trust, leaving her alone and with child. She soon gave birth to the infant Bragi. Some dwarves who were fond of Gunlod gave the newborn a magnificent harp and sent him out of the dark realm beneath the earth on one of their dwarven boats. The infant was thus shielded from the wrath of Suttung, who was outraged that his treasure had been stolen and his daughter defiled.

When the infant, who until this time had remained very still and lifeless, passed into the world above ground, his eyes opened and he picked up the harp and began playing beautiful music, the likes of which had never before been heard. The boat soon came to rest and Bragi took to his feet, walking among the many lands of Midgard, bringing song and joy wherever he went. Eventually he came across Idun, the goddess of youth, and the two deities fell in love; together, they were warmly welcomed into Asgard.

THIAZI AND THE THEFT OF IDUN'S APPLES

One day Odin, Loki, and Vili were struck with wanderlust. They left Asgard, hoping to find a bit of adventure. All day they walked throughout Midgard, but found little to pique their interest. When night began to fall and the earth began to quiet down they realized that the disquieting noises they heard were the rumblings from their empty bellies. Moving on ahead, Loki spied a herd of oxen. He quickly killed one of the beasts and returned with the fresh meat to the others, who had built a suitable fire.

They relaxed under the dusky sky as the meat cooked. The delicious smell of the roasting only increased their hunger. When their dinner looked fully cooked Odin pulled a joint out of the fire, but, biting into it, realized that it was still raw and cold in the middle. He put it back in the flames, thinking that his hunger must have made him impatient.

After more time had passed Odin again picked out a joint and took a bite, but still the insides were cold and red. Realizing that some form of trickery was afoot the three looked around their camp, searching for anything that might give a clue as to their bizarre situation. Their eyes soon came to rest on a massive eagle, sitting atop a tree, staring down at them. The eagle said he knew the solution to their problem but would only help them if they would let him have a portion of the meat. The gods agreed as their stomachs were doing their thinking for them.

The eagle flew down and stole away with both shoulder pieces and both rump pieces, the majority of the meat. It landed back on the tree and proceeded to feast. Incensed at the bird's gluttony, Loki picked up his staff and thrust it deep into the eagle's breast. With

Like the Aesir, the tribes of the North were famous for their wanderlust. This detail from a twelfth-century tapestry from Baldishol Church in Norway depicts a warrior in full battle gear as he roams in search of adventure.

a loud squawking the bird flew up into the air, taking the surprised Loki along with it, as his staff was too deeply imbedded to come out.

The eagle dragged the hapless Trickster all over Midgard, scraping him across rocks, dunking him into lakes and freezing streams, and slamming him against the faces of cliffs. Through all of this Loki held on, for he found that through some form of magic, his hands were stuck to his staff.

After hours of the bird's torturous flight, Loki had no choice but to plead with the eagle to stop battering him. The eagle looked down at Loki with dark eyes and said he would relent if Loki promised to bring him both Idun and her golden apples.

Loki knew from the request that the eagle had to be a giant in disguise and that the magic that glued his hands to the staff had to be of the giant's concoction. Loki didn't answer the request, since he knew that sacrificing Idun and her apples would bring old age, senility, and eventually death to the gods, himself included.

Frustrated, but determined to get the prize it sought, the eagle swooped down to earth at a frightening pace, smashing Loki's kneecaps and shins against a crag of brutally sharp rocks. Screaming in pain, the Trickster agreed to the bird's demands, and promised to bring Idun and her apples of youth out of Asgard in seven days.

As soon as the promise passed his lips his hands became unstuck from the staff and Loki found himself on the ground, bleeding and swollen and faced with an unpleasant task. After seven days of deliberation on how best to trick Idun out of Asgard, Loki paid the goddess a call at her palace. She received him with all the warmth and hospitality that one would expect from one who was never troubled. Loki immediately broke into his rehearsed speech. He told Idun how he had recently come across a tree in Midgard that produced apples that

looked very similar to the ones she always carried in her basket. And if the apples contained the same magic as hers the tree should be brought to Asgard and put under her protection. Idun agreed with Loki and asked to be shown the tree so a comparison could be made. She took her basket of apples with her so as to compare the fruits.

As soon as Idun and Loki set foot in Midgard the giant eagle rose up from a hiding place and grasped Idun and her basket in its talons. Off the eagle flew towards Jotunheim, just as Loki had suspected it would. The Trickster watched until he saw the bird land at the palace of Thrymheim, home of the giant Thiazi. There the bird transformed back into the giant and welcomed the befuddled Idun to her new home.

It didn't take long for the gods to feel the lack of Idun's youth-sustaining fruit. They began to age. Thor, once strong and powerful, now had trouble lifting Mjolnir. Freya's skin began to sag, causing her once-beautiful face to resemble that of a hag. Bragi found that he could no longer remember all the words to his wonderful songs. And even mighty Odin was having trouble keeping his mind focused. He also began to experience trouble holding his bladder.

Realizing that something must be done to remedy their situation, Odin called a meeting in Gladsheim. It took a while, but eventually all the Aesir hobbled in and took their seats. Odin shook his head, for the once-mighty Aesir now resembled a pitiful group of elderly fools. All, that is, except for Idun and Loki, who were not in attendance.

With the absence of Loki the gods immediately knew who was behind their troubles. Odin ordered that all of Asgard be searched until the Trickster was found. Loki was found relaxing in Idun's garden, incriminating him all the more. He was hauled before Odin and forced to reveal what had happened.

When the story was finished Odin decreed that Loki would travel to Jotunheim and retrieve Idun and her apples or he would be killed in a manner most fitting those who consorted with eagles. He would be spread out on a rock, face down. Incisions would be made down the length of his spine and then his entire rib cage would be pulled, intact, from his back, sprouting from his body like a pair of ghastly wings.

Loki immediately agreed to retrieve Idun. He asked Freya for her falcon cloak, and, donning it, took to the air, headed for Jotunheim. When he came to Thrymheim, Loki was lucky to find Thiazi out hunting and Idun unguarded in a little room. The Trickster spoke the runes that Odin had given him and Idun was turned into a nut. Loki then wrapped himself in Freya's cloak and, keeping a firm grip on Idun, took to the air once again, flapping furiously to get home before Thiazi returned and realized what had happened.

Thiazi returned shortly after Loki's departure and, finding Idun missing, realized that only the Aesir could have stolen her. He looked to the sky and saw Loki flying away. He quickly donned his eagle disguise and took to the air, determined to catch the god before he returned to Asgard.

From his seat on Hlidskialf, Odin could see Loki and Thiazi approaching. He noticed that Thiazi was gaining rapidly on the Trickster. Odin ordered that a massive pile of kindling be made just inside the walls of Asgard and that torchbearers stand at the ready. When the falcon-Loki passed over Asgard's wall Odin ordered the kindling to be lit. The dry twigs and branches caught fire immediately, flaring up to great heights and singing Thiazi's wings. With a flaming crash Thiazi fell to the ground inside Asgard, where he was quickly killed.

Having landed, Loki gently placed the nut on the ground and spoke the runes that would return Idun to her natural form. In a puff of mystical light the goddess appeared. She took one look at the old, haggard faces of her beloved friends and lost no time in distributing her apples to all of them. Soon, everything was back to normal in Asgard.

These gilt-bronze bird figurines of Swedish origin may have been brooches or harness mountings.

HEIMDALL—GUARDIAN OF ASGARD

One fine day, soon after the creation of the world, Odin was taking in the sea air along the beach. The wandering god came across nine giantesses relaxing in the cool sea air. He was so entranced by this nonet of gargantuan beauties that he decided to lie with each one, right then and there. So powerful was the passion generated among Odin and the giantesses that the nine women magically combined into one being, who subsequently gave birth to a son named Heimdall.

This detail from the Heimdall Cross slab is
a tenth-century Viking artifact from
the Isle of Man. Heimdall is pictured here
blowing Gjallar on the eve of Ragnarok.

Heimdall's nine mothers each had a different idea of what the child's diet should be, and hence he was fed on such different things as the steadfastness of the ground below his feet, the life-giving richness of the sea, the nourishing warmth of the sunlight, and so on. As a result of this diet Heimdall grew to full size in a few days, after which he traveled to Asgard to be reunited with his father. Upon his arrival he found the Aesir contemplating the wonders of the newly created bridge Bifrost, which spanned the chasm between Asgard and Midgard.

The Aesir were concerned that the giants might someday attempt to cross Bifrost and invade Asgard. They were wondering how to forestall such an invasion when their eyes fell upon the young Heimdall, noble in stature and pure of spirit. Unanimously the Aesir decided that Heimdall was perfectly suited to guard the rainbow bridge. The young son of Odin had eyes as sharp as an eagle's and ears so finely tuned that it was said he could hear the grass growing in Midgard. When he told the Aesir that he required less sleep than a bird, the position was his. Heimdall was appointed the guardian of Asgard. No one could enter or leave the realm of the Aesir without his knowledge.

Heimdall was outfitted accordingly. He was given the magical horn Gjallar, which he was to blow whenever he saw any hint of an approaching enemy. (It was this horn that would call the Aesir to battle for the last time during Ragnarok.) His palace was called Himinbjorg and was located at the highest point of Bifrost. From this location Heimdall could see every inch of the rainbow bridge. Gold Tuft, Heimdall's noble steed, sported a mane made of pure gold.

In depictions Heimdall is usually shown wearing brilliant white armor. This was highly suited to him, for he was considered by his fellow gods to be not only one of the most beautiful gods, but one of the kindest and wisest as well.

THE THEFT OF FREYA'S NECKLACE

Late one night Heimdall was distracted from his duties by the sound of soft, catlike feet heading in the direction of Sessrymnir, the palace of Freya. At first he thought nothing of it, figuring it was one of Freya's many cats returning from a late-night run. Heimdall's acute ears then heard the footsteps change into the buzz of a fly, betraying the fact that the visitor was no cat but some shape-shifting prowler. Focusing his magnificent eyes on Sessrymnir, Heimdall saw the fly revert back to its original shape at Freya's bedside. Loki was now hovering over Freya's sleeping body, his eyes riveted to Brisingamen, her beautiful necklace. His intentions were obvious. Heimdall chuckled to himself as he saw the look on Loki's face change when he noticed that the clasp of the necklace was underneath Freya's neck, impossible to get at without wak-

Heimdall and Bragi welcome a fallen warrior to Valhala; the newly slain mortal was no doubt escorted by the Valkyr in the background.

Loki, Brisingamen in hand, sneaks away from the sleeping Freya, unaware that Heimdall has seen the theft and is waiting for the Trickster to leave the bedroom.

sword a useless weapon. Not to be outdone, Heimdall transformed himself into a black storm cloud and sent sheets of rain heading towards the the flickering form of Loki. Seeing this, Loki changed his shape yet again, this time into that of a massive polar bear, with jaws large enough to catch the entire downpour. Before the first drop fell into Loki's ursine mouth, Heimdall shifted his shape into an equally huge bear and attacked Loki. The fight was furious, and soon Loki realized he was going to be beaten by his noble opponent.

Always the one to choose dishonor over death, Loki changed into a tiny seal the moment before Heimdall could snap his jaws around Loki's throat. Loki slipped from Heimdall's paws and started running away. By this point Heimdall was determined to bring Loki to justice in the most humiliating manner possible. He changed himself into an equally tiny seal and caught up with the fleeing coward. The two seals wrestled and fought until Heimdall had Loki in such a grip that the god of deception could neither move nor shapeshift. With a few choice curses directed at Heimdall, Loki relinquished Freya's necklace, and, when Heimdall released him, scampered off to clean his wounds and mend his pride. Necklace in hand, Heimdall quickly flew to Sessrymnir and returned Freya's precious treasure to her.

This incident was the first of many times Heimdall and Loki would spar. Their hatred for each other persisted right up until the two slew one another, during the apocalyptic conflict of Ragnarok.

ing her. His amusement turned into concern, though, when he saw Loki turn himself into a flea and jump onto Freya's side. The Trickster bit the sleeping goddess, making her turn over in her sleep, exposing the clasp to the night air and Loki's hands.

As soon as Loki had the necklace in his hands, Heimdall leapt from Bifrost to intercept the thief. Heimdall had never been able to stomach Loki; likewise, Loki had always found Heimdall to be distasteful. The two were direct opposites. Heimdall was good and just while Loki was evil and deceitful.

Heimdall stopped directly in front of Loki. By the look in the watchman's eyes Loki could tell his indiscretion had been discovered. He was about to launch into one of his lies proclaiming his innocence when Heimdall drew his sword from its scabbard, fully intent on decapitating the god of malice. Loki quickly spoke some runes and transformed himself into a flame, making Heimdall's

BALDER—GOD OF LIGHT AND TRUTH AND HODUR—GOD OF DARKNESS AND SIN

Balder, the god of light and truth, was the son of Odin and Frigga. He is typically depicted as the handsomest of all the Aesir. His flowing blond hair was thought to be the radiant beams of the summer sun, which warmed the earth and spirits of the northern races. His skill with runes and his tremendous knowledge of healing herbs made him a prominent deity during times of illness in Midgard. Of all the gods in the Norse canon, Balder was by far the most beloved.

Here, Balder and Nanna are resplendent in the sunshine that nurtures Midgard and symbolizes their innocence and beauty.

His palace was called Breidablik, where he lived with his wife, Nanna, a goddess of vegetation. Breidablik's most astounding feature was its golden roof, supported by towering pillars of solid silver. It was said that no untruth could pass through its doors.

Hodur, Balder's twin brother, was the exact opposite of his sibling. Where Balder exemplified light Hodur personified darkness. Where Balder personified innocence Hodur was the epitome of sin. Where Balder was able to see with the utmost clarity Hodur was totally blind.

One of the most important myths in the entire Norse canon concerns these two brothers. The myth tells of Balder's murder and how that event foreshadowed Ragnarok, the apocalypse.

THE DEATH OF BALDER

There came a time when Balder's sleep became terribly troubled. Night after night he lay in his bed in Breidablik, tossing and turning in a half-sleep, visited by terrible visions of dark and distasteful things. These dreams persisted for so long that Balder began to dread even the idea of going to sleep. Eventually, the lack of rest and the memories of the nightmares began to take their toll. The god who was usually the brightest and most joyful of all became dour and depressed, moping around Asgard, barely speaking to anyone.

It wasn't long before the Aesir took notice of the change in Balder's disposition. When asked about it he told them of his nightmares. The gods became greatly distressed. The dreams the god of light was having had to be

portents of great evil, they thought, since no untruth (and therefore no false visions) could pass through the walls of Breidablik. The gods knew that Balder's life was in great danger and that some method of forestalling his fate must be discovered.

They gathered in Gladsheim to discuss the problem. The Aesir racked their brains trying to think of every possible way in which Balder could meet his doom. They named every possible situation, weapon, disease, and being that could conceivably kill the most beloved of the gods. This catalog grew to astonishing proportions. When it was finished Frigga took it upon herself to travel to every corner of the nine worlds and get assurances from everything listed that they would never harm her son. She completed this task with little trouble.

Upon her return the gods again gathered in Gladsheim, this time for a celebration. It wasn't long before toasts to Balder's health and the crashing of drinking horns could be heard throughout Asgard. Soon, drunk with celebration and with mead, the Aesir decided to put Frigga's safeguards to the test. Picking up a tiny pebble, one of the gods flicked it at Balder's forehead. When asked if it stung, Balder responded that he had felt nothing. The pebble, remembering its oath to Frigga, had withheld its weight.

Growing in confidence the Aesir began experimenting with different weapons. From a pebble they graduated to a stone, then a boulder, then a dagger, then a sword, on and on, until even mighty Thor was hurling enormous axes at Balder. All of these items bounced off his skin, harmless as feathers.

Sulking in a dimly lit corner of Gladsheim, Loki determined to find something that could truly harm the god of truth. His eyes glowed with evil intent, a plan forming in his mind. With his characteristic slither, Loki left Gladsheim to mull over the possibilities.

Found in Sweden, this striking Viking spearhead—made of bronze with an incised silver hilt—demonstrates the synthesis of beauty and savagery common among the ancient Norse.

A few days later Loki had his plan. He transformed himself into a haggard old woman and made his way to Fensalir, Frigga's palace. When he got there he found the queen of the gods alone, taking a break from the ongoing celebration in Gladsheim.

Loki barged in, trying to be as obnoxious as possible. He made the long, warted nose he'd given himself run, creating quite a disgusting mess on the grungy frock he was wearing. In his grizzled voice he asked Frigga what all the commotion was throughout Asgard, referring to the cacophony emanating from Gladsheim. Frigga told the annoying hag that the revelers were celebrating the health of the god of truth. If this was the case, the old woman asked, why was someone there being tortured with all manner of weapon? Frigga then explained how she'd traveled the nine worlds, seeking assurances from everything that no harm would ever come to her son. With a wrinkled, bony finger, Loki picked at a boil and asked Frigga if she was certain she'd gotten such an assurance from everything. Now, being quite disgusted, and simply wanting the hag out of her sight, Frigga told her that there was in fact one thing she hadn't asked. That thing was the mistletoe, a shrub so young that she hadn't even bothered since she'd been certain it wouldn't have been able to understand her.

Loki kept up his revolting guise until Frigga rather forcibly asked the old woman to leave. Complying with her demands, the old woman left, heading in the direction of a patch of forest where mistletoe grew. Loki changed back to his original form, broke off a sizable branch, and sharpened one end into a fine point. With this in hand he walked back to Gladsheim.

Coming into the hall Loki made a beeline for Hodur. The blind god was standing over in a corner, propping himself up rather clumsily on a wall. He was not taking part in the fes-tivities due to his blindness. Loki, pretending to be kindhearted, told Hodur that it was a shame he had to be left out of the celebration. He offered not only to provide Hodur with a formidable-looking weapon but to guide his aim as well. Thanking Loki for his kindness, Hodur let himself be guided by the Trickster over to where the others were positioning themselves for the next throw. Grasping the mistletoe spear firmly in his hand, he let Loki guide his arm. He threw with all his strength. The staff pierced Balder through the chest, and without so much as a groan the god collapsed on the floor.

Having caused Balder's death, Loki sneaks away from the tumult, grinning maliciously.

The other gods were stunned. No one said anything; they simply looked at each other in befuddlement. But when they noticed the Trickster standing behind Hodur, still grasping his throwing arm, the Aesir knew the whole story. With a coward's speed Loki fled the great hall.

Then the lamentation began. The gods and goddesses could not restrain their grief. Where once Asgard echoed with the sounds of revelry, now there was the sound of mourning. Of all the gods only Odin knew the true consequences of this event, and because of this his mourning was the most soulful of all. He knew that with light and truth gone from the world Ragnarok could not be far off, when evil and death would gain hold, shaking the stability of the universe. The nine worlds would soon be nothing more than a smoldering pile of ashes.

Frigga, in her distress, called for some brave soul to travel to Hel's domain and ask for Balder's return to the land of the living.

Hermod, son of Odin and the messenger of the gods, offered his services. To aid him in his journey Odin lent him the use of the eight-legged Sleipnir. Without any goodbyes Hermod mounted Odin's steed and began the long journey to Niflheim.

As the sound of Sleipnir's hooves faded in the distance Odin ordered that Balder's body be taken to Breidablik and prepared for the funeral. He also ordered a great many trees felled so that a funeral pyre worthy of the slain god could be built. Down to Ringhorn, Balder's dragonship, the gods hauled their massive tributary gifts. On the ship's deck the pyre was built. When it was completed the bathed body was brought, dressed in the finest battle clothes, and placed atop the mountain of wood.

In keeping with tradition the ship was outfitted with the most luxurious worldly goods. Ornate tapestries, magnificent weapons, blazing golden objects—all were laid next to Balder's corpse. As the gods drew

This is a detail from a gilt-bronze weather-vane, an item that commonly adorned the prows of Viking longships. This weathervane, which dates from the tenth century, later decorated a church in Norway before finally finding a permanent home in a Stockholm museum.

mountain giantess Hyrrokin, who was so strong that she could launch the overladen craft singlehandedly.

Hyrrokin's arrival made many of the Aesir gape in horror. She was a terrifying vision, a monstrous form riding atop an equally huge wolf. The reins Hyrrokin held in her gnarled hands were made not of leather, but writhing serpents. She halted her mount and announced to the gods that she would help them launch the craft, but first her mount must be held fast, lest the ravenous wolf begin to devour all around him. Odin ordered four of his most savage berserks to hold the reins of snakes. Despite their insane strength, the berserks could not restrain the massive beast. Annoyed, Hyrrokin had to bind the monster's legs.

With a mighty shove the giantess pushed Balder's funeral ship into the water with an ear-splitting splash. So heavy was Ringhorn that the splash was heard throughout the nine worlds. With a heavy heart, Thor boarded Ringhorn and, while the pyre was being lit, held aloft Mjolnir, and spoke the magical words that would safeguard Balder's journey to Niflheim.

As Ringhorn sailed off to the horizon, the flames from the pyre gradually consumed the entire ship, making it sink into the sea along with the setting sun. Together the two created the most sadly beautiful sunset the Aesir had ever seen.

While mourning continued in Asgard, Hermod was nearing Niflheim. He rode over the dreaded bridge Giallar that spanned Giall, the river of the dead. Horse and rider jumped the massive entrance gates to Hel's domain with no trouble and galloped on to Hel's palace, deep in the heart of Niflheim, realm of the dead.

Upon entering Hel's dining hall Hermod saw both Balder and Nanna reclining on couches. The food in front of them was un-

nearer, each one paid their last respects to the slain god by presenting his corpse with their most prized possessions. Odin graced his fallen son with Draupnir, his self-replicating golden arm band. After he did this Allfather bent down and whispered something into Balder's ear. To this day Odin's words remain a mystery, although it has been speculated that he whispered the lone word "resurrection," for Odin possibly knew that his son would be reborn after the fires of Ragnarok destroyed the world. When Nanna approached to kiss her husband one last time, she fell down dead, the grief too much for her to bear. Her body was then laid next to his.

With all the preparations now completed the next step in the sad ceremony was to launch the ship, but due to its massive weight, the gods found Ringhorn to be immovable. Seeing the problem, Odin sent a messenger, Hermoch, to Jotunheim to ask the aid of the touched, as were the horns of mead set before them. Their spirits seemed as dead as their bodies. Hermod tried in vain to convince Balder that he should return to the land of the living. The dour spirit's only reply was a mournful look of sadness, telling Hermod that such things were now impossible.

Hermod approached Hel and told her of Frigga's plea to return her son to life. The goddess of death quietly listened, crossing her decayed legs. When Hermod finished Hel told him that she would release Balder if everything in the world, both animate and inanimate, shed a tear of grief for Balder. Acknowledging the bargain, Hermod again mounted Sleipnir for the journey back to Asgard. As he left Hel's murky realm, he was filled with the breath of hope. All of nature loved Balder, so he found it hard to imagine that Hel's request wouldn't be met.

Upon hearing the news Odin ordered four of his most trusted messengers to comb the four corners of the world and announce Balder's death. He was certain that when the news was heard, nothing in all of creation would be able to resist grieving. The messengers did their job well, and it wasn't long before everything, even the rocks and dirt of the earth, shed tears for the fallen god.

Returning to Asgard, the messengers saw one cave none of them had investigated before. Going inside they found it to be the home of the giantess Thok. When they told her of Balder's death she remained unmoved. When they asked her if she felt grief at Balder's demise she replied that she did not, that Hel could keep him forever for all she cared.

With dismal hearts the messengers returned to Asgard, carrying their sad news. When it was told that all but Thok had wept there was great depression throughout Asgard. It mattered little that no one had ever heard of Thok before. The conditions had not been met. Balder would remain dead.

In their mourning no one noticed the cunning glint in Loki's eye, a glint that revealed the true identity of the giantess Thok; the Trickster had struck again. The god of deception turned and left the others, doing his best to make it look like he was weeping.

Later, when the time for mourning ended, Odin determined that something should be done to avenge Balder's murder. He lay with his third wife, Rinda, and produced a son named Vali. Vali soon came to be called the Avenger, as it became clear that he was to be the one to seek justice for Balder's murder. He constantly carried both a small quiver full of arrows and a look of vengeance unfulfilled. One day, shortly after his birth, Vali came across Hodur and immediately slew the blind deity. By doing this, even though Loki was the true murderer, Balder's death was avenged in the eyes of the northern races. Balder and Hodur, now both dead, escaped the fury of Ragnarok.

After Vali's birth, Hodur began to have visions of Death, portents no doubt of his impending doom at the hands of Vali, the Avenger.

THE
REMAINING GODS

ew stories exist concerning the remaining gods in the northern pantheon,

but this does not mean these gods were inconsequential. Even though

hardly any stories about them survive, their personalities are an integral

part of the Norse canon and cannot be overlooked. The following pages

are devoted to descriptions of some but by no means all of the lesser Norse

deities. The gods who are discussed are Uller, Njord, Vidar, Aegir, Forsetti, Vali,

Hermod, and the Norns.

The counterparts to the Fates of Greek mythology, the
Norns controlled the history and destiny of human,
giant, and god. Pictured here at the root of Yggdrasil are
(from left to right) Urd, Verdandi, and Skuld.

The Vatnajokull
glacier in Iceland
is typical of the
forbidding environ-
ment that informed
the myths and legends
of the ancient Norse.

ULLER—GOD OF WINTER

The son of Sif and an unnamed frost giant, Uller was to the Norse not only the god of the winter months, but the god of hunting and archery as well. Since the winter months usually proved to be the time of many deaths for the Norse, Uller also held the position of god of the straw death.

Given his frost-giant lineage, it was only natural that Uller would feel most comfortable in the dreaded winter months that blanketed the northern regions for most of the year. During this time, it was believed that he took over command of Asgard from Odin, who would return to power when the first rays of sunlight warmed the earth. On one hand, the northern people considered him second in importance to Allfather. On the other hand, since Uller was not a very benevolent god—bestowing only ice, cold, and suffering upon Midgard—he was never as popular or beloved as Odin.

NJORD—GOD OF THE WINDS

After the war between the Aesir and the Vanir, the Vanir Njord, the god of summer, and the Aesir Vili exchanged places in accordance with the war pact. Njord and his children, Frey and Freya, took up residence in Asgard, and Vili moved to Vanaheim. Njord was thought to be a very handsome god, usually wearing a green tunic, which represented the growth of the summer months. As the god of calm, friendly weather, it was Njord who was typically invoked when a particularly fierce winter storm hit or an equally violent tempest blew in from the sea. His palace, Noatun, was

This detail from the Bryggen stick depicts an entire Viking fleet. Note the dragon heads and weathervanes that decorate the prows of the longships.

located near the seaside, supposedly so he could keep the temper of Aegir, the god of the oceans, in check.

Swans were considered sacred to Njord, because they first appeared each year at the beginning of summer. The playful seals that lived by the coast were also considered to be favorites of Njord, as they seemed to personify, with their playful nature, the pleasantness of the summer months.

VIDAR—THE SILENT GOD

Odin once lay with the giantess Grid. Together they produced a son, named Vidar, who was characterized not only by his magnificent strength but by the fact that he rarely, if ever, spoke. He represented the sheer force and quiet power of nature. He was destined to survive Ragnarok and be essential in the creation of the second universe. Vidar was de-

picted as a tall, handsome man, clad in armor, and always sporting a finely honed sword. He was also depicted wearing a sturdy pair of shoes, made of either iron or leather, that would protect his feet from the sharp teeth of Fenris, whom he would meet at Ragnarok to avenge his father's murder. It was believed that every piece of scrap leather that went unused in Midgard became part of Vidar's shoes, and hence Norse leather workers usually discarded their scraps with a very solemn and religious attitude.

AEGIR—GOD OF THE SEA

Aegir was the omnipotent lord of the oceans of the world. He was unique in that he belonged to neither the race of Aesir nor Vanir. He had existed long before those races came into being and would survive long after they had died.

Aegir was thought to be an old man, with long white hair and gaunt, tight skin stretched over his bony frame. He was not a kind god, but rather one who took perverse delight in overturning ships and drowning their crews. He and his wife, Ran (who was also his sister), lived for the moment when a ship, laden with men and treasure, would unknowingly pass above them, easy prey for their cruel and malicious hearts.

These two ornaments, which date from the late Bronze Age, were found in a funeral boat at a burial site in Denmark. It was a common practice among the ancient Norse to bury powerful warriors in a boat (or a boat-shaped plot) well equipped with weapons and valuables for the journey into the next world.

VALI—THE AVENGER

Vali was the son of Odin and Rinda. Not only avenger of Balder's death, Vali represented, along with Vidar, the undying forces of nature. Where Vidar stood for the quiet strength of nature, Vali was its undying spirit, the eternal light of life, the inner light and power that nourishes everything in nature. Vali was usually shown carrying a bow. From this bow he was able to shoot his magnificent, nourishing power all over Midgard.

ABOVE: **Here, Forsetti sits in judgment of a case involving two quarrelsome Aesir.**

RIGHT: **This sixth-century pendant, which is cast in the likeness of a Valkyr, was found in Sweden.**

FORSETTI— GOD OF JUSTICE AND LAW

Forsetti was the son of Balder and Nanna, the goddess of purity. With these two noble parents, Forsetti was automatically granted a seat in Gladsheim when he reached maturity. He was decreed the god of justice and given the wondrous palace Glitnir as his abode. Glitnir was very similar to Breidablik, the palace of his father, in that it had a silver roof supported by massive golden pillars.

Sitting on his throne in Glitnir, Forsetti was the supreme judge of Asgard. If any god had a quarrel with another, they would come before Forsetti to state their case. Upon hearing both sides of the story Forsetti would pronounce his judgment. His wisdom in such matters was so great that it was said no pair of disputants ever left Glitnir without respect and admiration for each other.

On Midgard Forsetti was always invoked before any trial or judgment was made. Of all the gods he was considered the most even-handed and levelheaded.

HERMOD—THE NIMBLE MESSENGER

The offspring of Odin and Frigga, Hermod was his father's trusty messenger. His quickness and agility were second to none. Often when

Odin was too busy, he would entrust Hermod with his terrible spear, Gungnir, with instructions to travel to Midgard where a battle was brewing. It was then Hermod's duty to sweep the mighty weapon over the battlefield, which would cause the bloodlust stewing inside the breasts of the warriors on both sides to boil, bringing on the murderous melee.

As Hermod often, under Odin's command, created the impetus for many battles, he was also known to aid the Valkyrs in transporting the slain from the field of battle to Valhala, where he was the leader of the Einheriar. Hermod's greatest moment was when he traveled to Hel to request the return of noble Balder's soul.

THE NORNS—
GODDESSES
OF FATE

The Norns were three sister goddesses who dictated and foretold the fate of the world, the gods, and man. Urd was the Norn who held sway over the past, and was usually shown as an old woman who continually looked over her shoulder into the very past she personified. Verdandi was the Norn of the present and was typically depicted as a youthful woman whose gaze always went forward, facing the present with a fearless attitude. These two sisters were generally considered to be helpful to both man and god. The third Norn was named Skuld, and she represented the future and every uncertainty the future held. In contrast with her sisters, Skuld was considered to be an unpredictable force with no particular love for either man or god; in addition, she had a very short temper. She was generally thought to be able to undo the prophecies and omens of the other two because of the

The Vikings and their northern contemporaries were a bloodthirsty lot, and funerals and funeral rites were a significant part of that culture. The advent of Christianity produced some interesting cultural juxtapositions, as can be seen in this detail from a tenth-century Anglo-Scandinavian cross in Middleton church, located in Yorkshire, England. Although the Scandinavian warrior is laid out in pagan fashion, his image is inscribed on the face of a cross.

fact that she alone had knowledge of the future. She was typically shown wearing a type of veil and clutching either an unopened book or a rolled-up scroll. Her gaze always fell directly opposite to that of Urd.

Every day the Norns would dutifully set to work weaving the web of fate, but at the end of the day Skuld had usually unraveled what Urd and Verdandi had woven. The result was that the future was never completely clear. The Norns were also in charge of watering and caring for Yggdrasil, tending to any broken limbs and making sure the dirt surrounding its roots was fresh and fully packed. The gods consulted the Norns constantly on important matters. The Aesir would come to the fountain of Urd, around which the Norns lived, and ask them for guidance.

XIII

RAGNAROK—THE APOCALYPSE

With Balder dead and Loki shackled, Odin knew the time of Ragnarok was not far off. Light and truth had been destroyed. And while evil had been imprisoned, Allfather knew that this shaky stability could not be maintained for long. He could feel the balance of the worlds shifting. He knew the end was near.

For too long the Aesir had tolerated Loki in their midst. Too often they had taken his advice and had had trouble because of it. Now, with Loki

This seventh-century artifact, called Sigurd's Helmet, comes from a pre-Viking grave site at Vendel, Sweden. A mortal hero, Sigurd was a favorite of Odin's, and in fact rode a steed (Greyfell) that was descended from Sleipnir.

banished to Midgard, Odin was certain Loki's evil was slowly seeping into the hearts and minds of men. With Balder dead, there was nothing with which to keep the spread of evil in check. Portents of doom were all that reached the eye of mighty Odin.

All too soon the malignant forces began to manifest themselves in Midgard. High on Hlidskialf Odin saw the men of earth wage war on each other, their hearts overtaken with evil and malice. He saw fathers cut down sons in fits of rage, sons slay their families under the blanket of night, brothers and sisters lie together, fathers and daughters bear children, mothers lust after sons. It was a time of metal on metal, sword blade on sword blade. Hatred and anger ran freely. Midgard ran red with blood. During this stage, mankind forgot the civilization it had created and reverted back to an earlier, more monstrous state.

After this age of weapons and blood came the time of Fimbulvetr. For three years the earth was blanketed in unending winter. The cold was unbearable. Ice and frost covered the world as far as Odin's eye could see. All of the creatures of the world starved. The lucky ones froze to death before starvation gripped them in its throes. It was a barren, desolate age, when the sun refused to shine and the earth refused to warm. During this hideous winter all that remained of people's humanity was discarded. The men of earth turned into little more than snarling, savage beasts, more akin to brutes than men. When the winter finally ended, all love and compassion was gone from the fields of Midgard. Only the blackest and most savage of hearts remained.

After the age of metal and the age of winter came the age of the wolf. The giantess Angrboda diligently fed Skoll and Hati, the wolves who pursued the sun and moon every day. Into their snarling jaws were thrust the bodies of those men who had killed their families and members of their clans. The bodies

of those who had taken liberties with their kin also found their final resting place between the jaws of these tremendous wolves. As the past years had been full of such brutality, Hati and Skoll never went hungry. In fact, they grew to such fantastic size and strength that they soon caught the heavenly orbs they had been chasing for so long. Skoll overtook the sun, chomping the chariot and its driver in his massive jaws, covering the Midgardian

snow with bright red gore. Hati likewise devoured the moon. After these losses, the stars lost their will to shine and the earth was covered in blackness.

This all-pervasive darkness not only killed the will of the stars, but destroyed the integrity of all magical bonds as well. All those imprisoned quickly found themselves free. Fenris felt Gleipnir drop around him, limper than unwoven flax. Loki felt his bonds dissolve and his freedom restored. The fires of vengeance flooded through these two evil beings, and their eyes glowed red with hate.

This darkness also gave Nidhogg, the serpent that lay deep in Niflheim curled around the root of Yggdrasil, the strength he needed. Nidhogg bit through the root, shaking the mighty ash tree to the heights of Asgard. The moment his teeth bit through, cocks crowed, alerting all to the fact that the end was near.

The age of blood and the age of winter, as described in the Norse canon, rendered the normally daunting Icelandic landscape completely uninhabitable by human and horse alike.

ABOVE: Heimdall blows Gjallar, rousing the Aesir, Vanir, and Einheriar to the final battle of Ragnarok. Gullinkambi can be seen just to the left of Heimdall echoing the call to arms.

OPPOSITE: This eighth-century picture stone from Sweden depicts a Viking ship under sail.

In Niflheim, Hel's blood-red rooster crowed its warning. Gullinkambi, the cock of Asgard, screeched his signal at the same time. From his perch high above Valhala, Gullinkambi could be heard throughout the realm of the noble Einheriar.

Apart from Odin, however, the only other Aesir to hear Gullinkambi's terrible portent was Heimdall. Like Odin on Hlidskialf, Heimdall was able to see all that went on in Midgard given his position on Bifrost, the bridge that separated the two worlds. After having seen the terrible age of blood and the blinding white age of Fimbulvetr, Heimdall knew the time had come for him to finally blow the sacred horn Gjallar. He did not do this lightly, for the music from Gjallar would rouse not only the Aesir but also the noble Einheriar for one final, valiant battle. Upon hearing the call to arms the Aesir and Einheriar quickly drew their swords, axes, and hammers and left the warm tables of Valhala. Through each of the five hundred and forty doors of the palace eight hundred noble souls emerged ready for

battle. They crossed Bifrost to Vigrid, the field where they all knew the final battle would take place.

The residents of Asgard were not alone in hearing the call to arms. Deep in the depths of the ocean, Jormungand, the serpent that encircled Midgard, heard the call and began to writhe and twitch, causing massive tidal waves and storms. Jormungand's movements brought the terrible ship Nagilfar to the surface. This ship was constructed of the nails of dead men, whose families had forgotten to clip them before entrusting their corpses to the flames of the funeral pyre.

As soon as Nagilfar broke the surface of the water, Loki, free from his torture, landed on its deck and steered it towards Vigrid. Along the way he was joined by his children, Fenris and Jormungand. The two evil brothers flanked the ship, Fenris devouring everything that came his way and Jormungand spewing poison everywhere. Where Nagilfar went only desolation was left in its wake. As the ship neared Vigrid, Loki caught sight of another

BELOW: This pre-Viking helmet, made of iron with a bronze crest running down to join the nose guard, dates from the seventh century. It was discovered in Vendel, Sweden.

OPPOSITE: Found in the northern part of the Isle of Man, this fragment of the Thorwald Cross depicts Fenris devouring Odin at the time of Ragnarok.

ship, sailing from Jotunheim, packed to the brim with giants, all of them armed and ready for the final battle. This second ship was steered by the hideous giant Hrym. Loki also saw, coming from Asgard, where they had just destroyed Bifrost, the flame giant Surtr and his children of fire, their eyes ablaze with the flames of wrath.

Loki beached Nagilfar on the shores of Vigrid and was delighted to see that his daughter Hel had emerged from a crack in the earth, bringing with her the terrible demon dog Garm. Nidhogg crawled out of the crack as well, bits of Yggdrasil's root still hanging from his reptilian jaws. It was a terrible sight when Nidhogg spread his wings and took to

the air, letting fall to the earth the countless corpses previously tucked away inside his leathery wings.

The forces were assembled. The final battle, the melee of Ragnarok, was about to begin. The two sides stared at each other for a long time. The Aesir, Einheriar, and the Vanir carefully studied the evil forces that stared back at them across Vigrid. Likewise, Loki, his minions, the flame giant Surtr, and the frost giants glared at the forces of good with hate and loathing in their eyes.

The field of Vigrid was soon filled with the cacophony of battle cries as the forces of good and the forces of evil commenced their attack. Odin fought Fenris. Thor faced Jormungand. Frey met Surtr. Tyr met Garm. Heimdall clashed with Loki. The Einheriar and the Vanir valiantly met Hel's undead army and the frost giants.

Odin's battle with Fenris was long and fierce, but eventually the terrible child of Loki

ABOVE: At Ragnarok, longtime enemies Heimdall and Loki finally destroy one another.

OPPOSITE: Dating from the twelfth century, this is a "stave church" of Norweigan make. These churches, although used for Christian worship, were of pagan design. To ward off the forces of evil, these churches were decorated not only with crosses but with dragon's heads as well.

RIGHT: This seventh-century brooch of Swedish origin represents Jormungand, the world-encircling serpent.

creature lay dead at Thor's feet, the Thunderer staggered back, overcome by the venom the snake had saturated him with during their battle. After only nine steps, the Thunderer likewise fell dead.

No sooner had Frey and Surtr clashed weapons than the god of sunshine regretted the fact that he had given away his magical fighting sword to his faithful servant Skirnir. Although the battle between them was long, Surtr's fiery blade proved to be the death of noble Frey.

Tyr and the hideous Garm fought long and hard, and fell together in a heap, both of them dead. Likewise, longtime enemies Loki and Heimdall, their mutual dislike for each other burning strongly in their hearts, slew one another after a hideously brutal melee.

When the sounds of battle had faded and Vigrid was covered with nothing but corpses, Surtr, who alone had survived, flung his massive flaming sword around his head, throwing the fires of Muspellsheim into every corner of the nine worlds, covering everything with devouring flame. All was destroyed. The palaces of Asgard and of Jotunheim, the mortal villages of Midgard, and the dank depths of Hel were all consumed by Surtr's cleansing fire. The world was dead. And so it sank beneath the enveloping waves of the sea.

swallowed Allfather in one gulp. Thus transpired the death of Odin, King of the Aesir. But Fenris had no time to savor his victory; Vidar, Odin's son, quickly leapt at the gigantic wolf and stretched the beast's foul jaws so wide that they scraped both earth and heaven. With a mighty crack Vidar finally ripped Fenris in two.

Thor and Jormungand were equally matched, but it was soon proven that Mjolnir was mightier than the giant serpent. As the

THE
NEW UNIVERSE

The ancient Norse believed that when everything had been destroyed, the earth would rise again, out of the life-giving sea, fresh and green once more. This occasion would give Sol's daughter, who was born before her mother was eaten by Skoll, the inclination to take up the reigns of her mother's chariot and once again make the sun travel across the sky. This new unflawed sun would not burn the daughter of Sol, so no heat shield was needed. Soon its healing rays touched every corner of the new world, creating abundant

This ninth-century sculpture of a Viking warrior was found in Oslo, Norway. As the majority of these sculptures were made of wood, few specimens have survived to the present day.

life. Yggdrasil, which survived Ragnarok, grew green and fruitful once again, its roots implanted deeply in this new and fertile earth, creating a cosmic stability that far surpassed that of the old universe. When they noticed the world turning green once again the eyes of the two surviving humans peeked out from their hiding place within Yggdrasil. The woman was named Lif, the man Lifthrasir. The pair climbed out of their sanctuary and began building their lives anew in a world that had been reborn from the ashes of the old order.

Lif and Lifthrasir were not the only beings to survive the fires of Ragnarok. Vidar, the slayer of Fenris, and Vali, the avenger of Balder, somehow escaped Surtr's flames. These two personifications of the indefatigable spirit of nature were met by Magni and Modi, the sons of Thor, on the plain of Idavoll, where once stood Asgard. Magni and Modi had salvaged their father's hammer from the fires of Ragnarok, and with their strength, Mjolnir's power, and Vidar and Vali's energy they built a new heaven. They were joined there by the twin brothers Balder and Hodur, who had been given new life, resurrected in the new world with their past differences resolved. There would be no place in this new universe for spiteful grudges and vendettas among the few remaining deities. The two reincarnated brothers met each other and embraced.

The only other Aesir to survive was Vili, brother of Odin, who had, along with Odin and Ve, created the first world out of Ymir's gigantic corpse. These seven gods sat on Idavoll and remembered their dead kin with

the honor due fallen heroes. They soon discovered, much to their joy, that the gaming fields of the old gods had survived the ravages of the apocalypse. In some versions these fields contain magnificent golden chessboards; in others, they are where the Aesir used to throw their golden dice in games of chance. Either way, the new gods' discovery of this treasured field would be a constant reminder of the glory and honor of their fallen brothers and sisters.

The seven deities soon restored what once was Asgard. The finest palace they called Gimli. It was built higher than any palace of old Asgard had ever been. Here the gods would reside, overseeing the goings-on down below. The old evils had been destroyed. The world was fresh again, unspoiled, unstained. While the ending of the old world had been bathed in fire and fury, the beginning of the new world was awash in sunshine and the promise of a bright future.

BIBLIOGRAPHY

Anderson, R.B. *Norse Mythology*. Chicago: S.C. Griggs, 1891.

Branston, Brian. *Gods of the North*. London: Thames & Hudson, 1955.

Carlyon, Richard. *A Guide to the Gods: An Essential Guide to World Mythology*. New York: Quill, 1989.

Comte, Fernand. *Mythology*. Edinburgh: Chambers, 1991.

Cotterrell, A. *A Dictionary of World Mythology*. New York: Perigee, 1979.

Craigie, William A. *The Icelandic Sagas*. Cambridge: Cambridge University Press, 1913.

Crossley-Holland, Kevin. *The Norse Myths*. New York: Pantheon, 1980.

Davidson, Hilda Ellis. *Gods and Myths of Northern Europe*. London: Penguin, 1990.

———. *Pagan Scandinavia*. New York: Praeger, 1967.

Eliot, Alexander. *The Universal Myths: Heroes, Gods, Tricksters and Others*. New York: Meridian, 1990.

Evans, Bergen. *Dictionary of Mythology*. New York: Laurel, 1970.

Gelling, Peter, and Hilda Ellis Davidson. *The Chariot of the Sun and Other Rites and Symbols of the Northern Bronze Age*. New York: Praeger, 1969.

Graham-Campbell, James. *The Viking World*. New Haven: Ticknor & Fields, 1980.

Guerber, H.A. *Myths of the Norsemen From the Eddas and Sagas*. New York: Dover, 1992.

———. *Myths of the Northern Lands*. New York: American Books, 1895.

Hamilton, Edith. *Mythology*. Boston: Meridian, 1989.

Haviland, Virginia. *Favorite Fairy Tales Told In Norway*. Boston: Little, Brown and Co., 1961.

Kaster, Joseph. *Putnam's Concise Mythological Dictionary*. New York: Perigee Books, 1990.

King, Cynthia. *In the Morning of Time: The Story of the Norse God Balder*. New York: Four Winds Press, 1970.

Leach, Maria, and Jerome Fried, eds. *Funk and Wagnalls Standard Dictionary of Folklore, Mythology, & Legend*, 2 Vols. New York: Funk and Wagnalls, 1949–50.

Robinson, Spencer H. *The Encyclopedia of Myths & Legends of All Nations*. London: Kaye & Ward, 1962.

Wilson, David M. *The Vikings and Their Origins*. New York: A & W Visual Library, 1980.